DRAGONS' DEN

THE PERFECT PITCH

DRAGONS' DEN

THE PERFECT PITCH

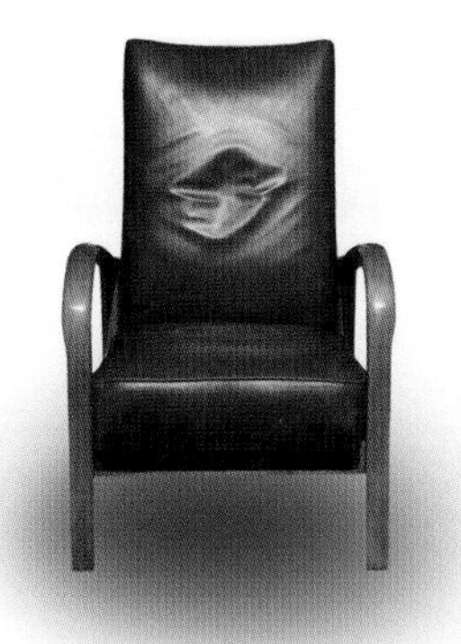

HOW TO WIN OVER AN AUDIENCE

PETER SPALTON

Collins

A division of HarperCollins*Publishers*
77-85 Fulham Palace Road, London W6 8JB
First published in Great Britain in 2010 by HarperCollins*Publishers*
1

A catalogue record for this book is available from the British Library.
ISBN 978-0-00-736427-5

Dragons' Den
Created by Nippon Television Network Corporation
This book is produced under licence from 2waytraffic, a Sony Pictures Entertainment company/CPT Holdings. Dragons' Den and all associated logos, images and trade marks are owned and controlled by 2waytraffic.

Produced by Thameside Media
www.thamesidemedia.com

Printed and bound by Graficas Estella, Spain

ABOUT THE AUTHOR

Peter Spalton CMC is a professional speaker and business consultant whose clients include multinationals, public bodies, private companies and family businesses. He is a member of the Professional Speakers' Association and has held senior marketing positions in ICL, Ericsson and Nokia. He is the author of *Marketing Secrets* in the Business Secrets series, also published by HarperCollins, and co-author of *Dragons' Den: Grow Your Business*.

CONTENTS

FOREWORD

FROM DRAGONS' DEN HOST EVAN DAVIS

When BBC executives first saw a pilot of a new programme called Dragons' Den, they loved the show but were concerned about the name. They said the words *"Dragons' Den"* didn't tell viewers what they will see. "What about a name that would make more sense to a reader of the *Radio Times*?" they asked. Fortunately, no-one could agree on a better title so the original stuck.

But one of the least bad alternatives that had been floating around was *"Life's a Pitch"*. That did have the merit of not just telling you the programme was about pitching, but also of capturing the essence of a modern existence: as long as we are awake and in company, we seem to be selling something. A product, an idea, or even ourselves, whether it be to an employer or a bureaucrat, to a spouse or partner, or even to a class of school children.

Maybe indeed this is our evolutionary destiny. We differ from chimpanzees in that we have powers of persuasion, and we have to use them to survive. Well this book is a guide to one important aspect of persuasion: the formal pitch.

I should point out that it is not specifically a guide to pitching in front of the Dragons (which is far more challenging than most of us will ever have to cope with). It is about the pitches that occur every day and everywhere in commercial life around the country.

For me, an important point emerges from these pages (particularly in Commandments 3, 4 and 6). It is that to make a good pitch, you need a good understanding of what it is you are pitching. If you don't know what your central message is, don't expect to be able to sell it very successfully. And if you are unclear as to what problem your product solves, you won't just run your business badly, you won't pitch it well either.

I would even argue that you can use pitching as a technique for sharpening your thinking. Even if you don't have to make a pitch, maybe you can clarify your thoughts by preparing one!

I hope you'll find the book useful and that it will make you think not just about how to deliver a formal sales pitch, but also about how you organize your thoughts and present yourself whenever you need to convey a message to other people.

Evan Davis

COMMANDMENT 1

USE THE POWER OF PRESENTATION

What is pitching all about?

DRAGONS' DEN highlights the power of presentation. What marks out some business ideas as better than others? What persuades Dragons to hand over great wads of their own cash to some entrepreneurs, while others who enter the Den have to walk away without a penny? Pitching is an art. And it's an art that any would-be entrepreneur needs to learn, whether they're applying to go on Dragons' Den or setting up meetings with investors or selling to potential clients. This book shows you how to craft the perfect pitch and succeed where others fail.

WHAT IS A PITCH?

If you look up 'pitch' in the dictionary, you'll see it is defined along the lines of: 'A persuasive sales talk or bid to gain a contract or some other business deal'. The key words are 'sales' and 'persuasion'. Many people are frightened by the word 'sales', but as a budding entrepreneur, you'll already be selling your ideas most of the time and are probably good at it. This book will show you how to turn a sales talk into a proper, persuasive pitch. The skills you learn from this book will enable you to succeed in any environment where you are giving a presentation, but our case studies are focused on Dragons' Den-style pitches to potential investors.

If you're a start-up business, your pitch will be a presentation of your business plan, maybe to a group of bankers. If you've been

MIKE COTTON OF DDN *gave an exemplary pitch for investment in the Den in Series 6. He outlined the first market in the UK in terms of potential customer numbers and the even more appealing bigger market throughout Europe. He demonstrated the profitability of the product and made it clear that his remit for equity negotiations was limited. It gave the Dragons a clear target and each had to think about what they could offer in terms of experience and contacts to compete with the other Dragons. It put Mike in a strong negotiating position* *(see pp226–7).*

trading for some time, you'll argue a case for investment with a business development plan. The shape and content of both types will be similar, with only the emphasis and decision criteria being different.

The key thing to remember is that pitching isn't begging or pleading, but selling. Instead, you should adopt the attitude that you're offering an opportunity that they'd be foolish to refuse.

GUY PORTELLI IS A SCULPTOR WHO WENT INTO THE DEN ASKING FOR INVESTMENT *in a series of works he wanted to exhibit, initially in London. He kept the pitch on a firm business footing, describing his work only in the simplest of terms and concentrating his presentation on the commercial facts and figures of the venture. It left the Dragons in no doubt as to the profit potential of the deal. Find out how Guy got on in the case study on pp54–5.*

A PITCH CAN HAVE A NUMBER OF FORMS, BUT IT HAS ONLY ONE OBJECTIVE. TO PERSUADE SOMEONE TO BUY YOUR IDEA.

OUTCOME OF A PITCH

In the Dragons' Den, a pitch results in either an offer of investment or a rejection on the spot. In other settings, you may have to wait for a few days or weeks before you get an offer or rejection. Assuming your pitch results in an offer of investment, there will follow a due diligence period, usually a month, when the investor will rigorously check your figures and your background (see also pp224–5).

IN THE DRAGONS' DEN *entrepreneurs first give a presentation about their business, stating how much investment they are seeking and how much equity they are offering in return. There then follows a questioning session in which the Dragons explore the business further, ascertaining the financial condition of the current business, the opportunity for growth in the near future and looking for any potential pitfalls in an investment deal.*

MICHAEL NORTH *(right) was one such entrepreneur who went on Dragons' Den in Series 6, seeking investment for his fledgling olive oil club (see pp160–1). For a while, Michael struggled to get across the idea that, because olive production is seasonal and the seasons vary in different parts of the world where olives are grown, he would be able to supply olive oil only as and when the seasons dictated rather than on a regular basis of, say, one bottle per month. The bigger hurdle, however, was convincing the Dragons that selling oil in this way was a viable business proposition, regardless of how good it tasted.*

THE IDEAL FORM OF PITCH

This book is called *The Perfect Pitch*, and the type of pitch that it focuses on has three essential elements:

- **A PRESENTATION (ALLOW ABOUT 20 MINUTES IF POSSIBLE)**
- **A QUESTION AND ANSWER SESSION**
- **A TAKE-AWAY PACK WITH FACTS, FIGURES AND FINANCIAL INFORMATION**

Although there are other forms of pitching (see below), the type of presentation described above is best because it gives you the greatest opportunity to control the proceedings and chance to shine. This is because the pitcher stands in a position of power at one end of the room, facing the audience. Even though the audience might sit around the table, it's you as the pitcher who's in the spotlight and has the control – and the pitch is all about power.

OTHER FORMS OF THE PITCH

Sometimes people will ask you to pitch in a different way, such as in a letter, or invite you to have a chat over lunch, or summon you to a boardroom meeting. We'll take a look at these forms now, but generally you should avoid pitching in these ways because without the presentation element it is very difficult to be successful.

- **THE LETTER PITCH.** These days writing a letter as a sales pitch has almost become a forgotten art, although there are professional copywriters who will spend days crafting a successful letter. The nearest the rest of us get to doing a pitch by letter is when applying for a job. The job application is like a pitch – the CV is the same as the take-away pack with all the facts and figures about you; the letter explains why you are the best candidate; and the interview is where you lay out your argument for the job and respond to their questions. However, a letter on its own falls far short of a face-to-face presentation.

- **THE SEEMINGLY INFORMAL LUNCH PITCH.** An invitation to pitch over lunch may be face-to-face and seem less scary than a formal presentation, but it is even more precarious than the letter pitch. Not only do you have to worry about where you're going and what you're going to eat, but you also have to think about whether you're going to have a drink. It's best if you can leave the choice of venue to your audience because it poses a real quandary. For instance, do you pick somewhere cheap and practical to show that you don't waste money? Or do you pick somewhere famous and expensive to impress them? You might want to settle for somewhere between the two – maybe a slightly unusual restaurant so you come across as someone who has confidence and style. Then there's the challenge of talking while you eat and coping with interruptions from waiters. But the main problem with the informal lunch pitch is cultural. In Britain we tend to pussyfoot around, make small talk and wait nervously for the other party to talk business, whereas in America they openly accept that they're there for business, so

CASE STUDY **FROM SERIES 7 EPISODE 5**

MYDISH

Carol Savage made a successful pitch for her online business, MyDish, a recipe-sharing website for people looking for inspiration or to swap and share recipes.

In her pitch, Carol carefully stressed the familial and intimate side of the site (gran's old recipes, personal favourites, and so on), which is an important component of community-based websites. She also described it as a kind of iTunes for recipes, subtly equating it with a proven online business.

Having built this platform of credibility, she then moved on to the financial prospects, introducing a variety of revenue streams, some of which were already providing income. Despite a great deal of money having already been invested (£600,000) and break-even point still a long way off, Carol remained persuasive in her arguments, and projected exciting turnover figures for the next three years, extrapolated from the growth in visits to the site in relation to the income currently being generated.

For a business yet to prove its profitability, it was a redoubtable pitch.

CAROL RECEIVED *the £100,000 investment she'd pitched for from Deborah Meaden in exchange for 15% equity.*

get down to it straight away. In parts of Scandinavia a pitch can take place over a beer or in the sauna. In most countries, however, lunch and the sauna are great places to gain support for your deal and for lobbying, but they're not really for pitching. Avoid the lunch pitch if you can.

- **THE BOARDROOM TABLE PITCH.** Finally there's the pitch around the boardroom table. At first sight it seems similar to the type of presentation described earlier as ideal. But usually it's about control and status. The decision maker is in the superior place at the head of the table and the pitcher is put on the back foot in a subordinate position at the end. The decision maker has the power and the pitcher can't easily use props and more often than not loses control of the flow. The boardroom table is not for pitching, it's for negotiating.

UNDERSTAND THE BALANCE OF POWER

So now you can see the problems with other forms of pitches, let's get back to the ideal pitch, in which you give a presentation, followed by a question and answer session, then you give out a take-away pack.

During the presentation part you are on a stage and control the proceedings. During the question and answer session the power flips between the person who asks the question and you when you give the answer. If you answer clearly and confidently you are still in command. Finally, when you hand out the take-away pack you relinquish control and pass power to the people in the audience.

You always need to bear in mind that even though the audience has the power to reject your pitch, you have the power to win them over. I know it sounds a bit silly, but as the pitcher you have authority because of your position in the room and credibility because of your knowledge and expertise.

DURING CAROL SAVAGE'S PITCH *(see p19), she was questioned thoroughly about income revenues from a website business, about the site's unique visits and returning visitor numbers, and not least about the amount of investment already residing in the business. She never remained on the back foot long, though, and for every question was able to counter with figures that indicated there was opportunity for her business to grow and her website to develop further functionality and a burgeoning network of users.*

UNDERSTAND THE EMOTIONS IN THE ROOM

At the end of the day, assuming your idea is basically sound, your audience's decision may be based largely on emotional factors and be totally self-centred. It might hinge on things like their own ego, ambition and desire factored by how much they trust you.

Nobody can predict the future; what you must do is convince them that the risk they take is minimal. Show them what's in it for them and demonstrate that you're the person that can make it happen.

Of course you'll be nervous, but a good pitch should be fun and enjoyable. In Commandment 9 we'll talk about how you can convert your nervous energy into enthusiasm.

IN KAY RUSSELL'S PITCH FOR PHYSICOOL *(see p140–1), she forgot to say in her introduction just what the product was. A bemused Theo looked at the packaging and assumed that it was a drink. Kay acknowledged the fact that she had forgotten this key piece of information, and in so doing brought a note of levity to the Den. Humour in a pitch won't always play well (see Ladderbox on p71), but a moment like this can just ease a bit of tension. Unrehearsed as it was, it revealed a level of nervousness in Kay that in fact indicated that she was treating the situation seriously.*

Even though you are selling and want something from the audience, you don't have to be sweet and nice. In some ways you must show them that you're not that hungry for the deal. There's also a lot to be said for coming across as determined and even a bit ruthless – but not arrogant or pigheaded. They need to be reassured that you have enough determination to deliver results. After all it's their money that's at risk. You must also demonstrate that you have enough confidence and see them as potential partners.

Confidence is often shown by simplicity. Advertising people call it white space. If you're confident about your message, you don't need to fill the whole advert with words and pictures. Pitches with a simple, clear message actually say it all.

SIMPLE IS BEST. IF YOU CAN GET THE ESSENCE OF YOUR PITCH ON A SINGLE SHEET OF A4, THEN YOU'LL HAVE A WINNER.

TAKE A HELICOPTER VIEW

In Commandment 2 we'll look at the different types of audience and how you can match your pitch to their needs. But first you need to understand that pitching is about *you*. The techniques for giving a good presentation are fairly easy to learn and just take practice. We'll cover them later. Before you start to think about what you're going to say, though, you need to stand back and look at what you're trying to achieve. In fact, at this point you're not writing a pitch but thinking about the four 'Ws'.

'THE FOUR WS'

- **WHAT** do you want to achieve?
- **WHERE** are you going to do the pitch?
- **WHO** will be there?
- **WHICH** one thing do you want them to take away?

“ A PESSIMIST SEES THE DIFFICULTY IN EVERY OPPORTUNITY; AN OPTIMIST SEES THE OPPORTUNITY IN EVERY DIFFICULTY ” WINSTON CHURCHILL (1874–1965)

WHAT DO YOU WANT TO ACHIEVE?

Is this your initial pitch, with your goal being simply to get to the next meeting? Are you pitching to someone you would like as a partner? Is it a potential client, and you want to be on their preferred supplier list? Or is it an investor who might be looking for an exit strategy and earn-out in three to five years? See Commandment 2 for more about pitching to different audiences.

WHERE ARE YOU GOING TO DO THE PITCH?

You need to know the location, the time of day, how long you'll have and what sort of facilities will be available. Think about how you will handle it if it's in their offices, on neutral ground or on your own premises, if you're already trading. Will you get only one shot or will you have a chance to wine and dine them and show them around your facilities first? This will have a bearing on the content of your pitch. You'll also need to know if the room has presentation equipment. You must have answers to all these things before you can even think about what sort of presentation you're going to give.

WHO WILL BE THERE?

It's important that you find out who is going to attend your pitch. You might know them personally, or know someone else who does.

Do some research on them so you know more than just their job title. Try and find out what they specialize in, how much they know about you and whether they know anything about your market, what they've invested in before and what their 'hot button' is.

WHICH ONE THING DO YOU WANT THEM TO TAKE AWAY?

All good pitches have one memorable point, for example it could be a slogan (e.g. the olive oil pitch below) or it could be something financial. Imagine what you want the members of your audience to feel and remember when they leave the room. You may not be able to think clearly about this yet, but at some point you will need to.

THINK OF MICHAEL NORTH AGAIN, *with his passion for quality olive oil. Whatever else came of the pitch, he wanted to get across the idea of "seasonal, fresh olive oil". He even stopped in his pitch to introduce those four words – words that he told the Dragons they would never have heard together before.*

When you've taken the helicopter view, you can start to think about the shape and structure of the pitch. Don't start planning your speech at this point, though. Instead, start off by considering how to appeal to the emotions of the audience and pull them into the opportunity you're offering them.

SEDUCE THEM AND SHOW YOUR PASSION

You need to seduce your audience and demonstrate your passion for the product in the presentation part of your pitch. This is how you appeal to their emotional side. It sounds difficult, but if you are passionate about your idea and channel your nerves into enthusiasm, you will carry your audience with you. In many ways your idea or product doesn't have to be the best. But you must convince your audience that you can deliver what you promise. You will win them over if you make them feel they mustn't miss out on your offer.

IN LABAN ROOMES'S PITCH *for his gold-plating business, now known as Goldgenie, the entrepreneur had almost run out of road – all but one of the Dragons had decided not to invest. Then Laban made one last plea, a passionate speech listing the things he had achieved and expressing his self-belief and desire to succeed. Known for being an investor in people, a smiling James Caan was seduced. "I love things that sparkle," he said, and Laban certainly sparkled.*

... YOU NEED TO SEDUCE THEM WITH A SOFT-SELL. Think how politicians and advertisers seduce us with their words and images every day. We all have the power within us to seduce someone. It's just that some people have developed this power to a higher level. Sometimes it's known as a soft-sell and it's naturally much more effective than going like a bull at a gate with an aggressive hard-sell. The soft-sell takes time, but it does have the power to enthral people and draw them into your pitch.

... **SEDUCTION IS BETTER THAN LOGIC.** The alternative to the soft-sell is to sell through a logical argument. But that is hard because the audience has to buy into logic completely and you can easily lose them. With a soft-sell you capture them if you use words and images that play on their basic emotions. You want them to feel stirred and uplifted. In this context it's all about how you paint a positive picture of the future and use action words. You mustn't appear to be selling hard because you'll come across as manipulative and they will start to get suspicious. As the well-known saying goes, "If it sounds too good to be true, it probably is."

"PASSION IS THE ONLY THING WHICH ALWAYS PERSUADES"

FRANÇOIS DE LA ROCHEFOUCAULD, MEDIEVAL WRITER

... **YOU'RE SELLING A PROMISE.** It's all about the structure of your pitch, the clarity of your message and the image you portray with your personality and props or visuals. You're selling a promise, and they have to believe that you will be able to make it happen.

... **OR IMAGINE IT AS A MARRIAGE PROPOSAL.** You must convince them to enter into a long-term relationship with you. It needs to be a memorable moment and you need to come across as trustworthy and enthusiastic.

... **OR THINK OF IT AS THEATRE.** You're an entertainer. Not a comedian, magician or song and dance act, but somebody who also has the 'wow' factor. Understand that people will buy into your passion and enthusiasm.

If you want some real-life examples, look to the popular presenters of documentaries and lifestyle programmes on television. Dr Brian Cox, Ray Mears and Jeremy Clarkson, for example, passionately believe in their subjects, and it's infectious. Many of the celebrity chefs, such as Jamie Oliver, Rick Stein and Nigella Lawson, also exude enthusiasm and a passion for what they do.

" MAKE SURE THAT YOU ARE PASSIONATE ABOUT THE PRODUCT AND ENSURE THAT IT IS ACTUALLY REAL AND SUSTAINABLE "

THEO PAPHITIS, DRAGON

SEDUCE WITH THE SHAPE OF YOUR PITCH

There are two schools of thought for the shape of your pitch: unwrapping it like a present or building it up like a jigsaw.

THE BIRTHDAY PRESENT

This approach is like giving the audience a birthday present wrapped in pretty paper with a big bow. So you show them the whole thing and slowly unwrap it so eventually they see what's hidden inside.

Think of this approach as, "First tell them what you want, tell them why and then what they get in return."

THE JIGSAW

The jigsaw is where you show them one piece at a time and gradually build up to the complete picture.

This is, "Tell them you have an exciting opportunity and then tell them what it's about, what you want and what they get in return."

THINK OF ENTREPRENEURS *such as Sarah Lu of Youdoo (from Series 5) and Tony Earnshaw of UK Commercial Cleaning (in Series 7): very different businesses, but in their respective pitches both individuals showed a genuine passion for what they were doing. They had belief in what they were doing, goals about what they wanted to achieve, and they were prepared to invest in those objectives using their time and money. It was their entrepreneurial passion that impressed the investors as much as the businesses – more than the businesses in fact.*

Both approaches are very seductive. Which one you choose will depend on the amount of time you have, your personal style and the type of audience. Steve Jobs of Apple gives brilliant

STEVE SMITH'S PITCH FOR TRUECALL *(pp218–19) was going reasonably well but was by no means in the bag when he revealed the extent of his past successes. He had built up and sold two previous businesses for several million pounds, instantly winning him respect and credibility in the Den.*

PETER IN PARTICULAR *then had to think hard about what deal he could offer to gain the investment opportunity that Steve presented.*

presentations of Apple's products, all of which are designed to be objects of desire and seduce the customers, whereas Bill Gates of Microsoft talks technology and may come across as wooden to many non-technical people.

ESTABLISH YOUR CREDIBILITY

Credibility is a combination of expertise or knowledge and trust. If you've done it before in business, it's not a problem as your reputation says it all. Richard Branson has credibility because he's done it many times with the Virgin brand. So do the Dragons.

Presuming you're not in their league, then you may need to build your credibility from scratch. That's all about how you come across – your confidence, how you answer questions and the content of your presentation. So on one level you need to appeal to their heart with an emotional element and on the other level you need to appeal to their head with both logic and reasoning.

“ I COVERED TWO PRESIDENTS, LBJ AND NIXON, WHO COULD NO LONGER CONVINCE, PERSUADE, OR GOVERN, ONCE PEOPLE HAD DECIDED THEY HAD NO CREDIBILITY ”

HELEN THOMAS, AMERICAN JOURNALIST

APPEAL TO THEIR HEAD

We recognize things by their structure. Think about an item in a newspaper. It has a headline to draw us in and the news story is in the first paragraph. The rest of the piece provides us with more and more information leading to a conclusion. Sometimes it's for entertainment, sometimes it's to inform us of what's going on. At other times it's to persuade us to a particular point of view. The important thing is that the structure feeds into the logical and reasoning part of our brain. This approach is commonly called 'appealing to the head'.

Since you have to assume they know nothing about you and your idea, or the market, you need to take some time to explain what it's all about. So it's best to have a 'problem-solution-action' structure.

1. **PROBLEM.** Background information that describes the problem your idea will solve. In other words, the market need.

2. **SOLUTION.** Information about your idea, or the solution to the problem. How it satisfies the market need and why people would want to buy it.

3 **ACTION.** The size of the opportunity which you'll need to translate into financial terms such as sales. This section is about a realistic forecast with specific time-scales.

4 **PROJECTED OUTCOME.** What you've achieved so far and what you have in hand for the next few months. What you want from them to make it happen and what they can expect in return.

The basic structure of your presentation is always the same. Only the emphasis will change according to how much your audience knows about your market. During the presentation you will need to give them compelling evidence that you're not talking out of the top of your head. This is the knowledge or expertise part of your credibility and most of it will come from the way you handle questions and the content of your take-away pack. We look at all these issues in more detail in Commandments 3, 4 and 6.

APPEAL TO THEIR HEART

Words are two-a-penny and you can't hope to convince investors by your argument alone. They have to believe that you have the energy, motivation and determination to deliver what you say you will. They have to trust you, and that's the other element of credibility. You must tell them what you've done so far and what other things you have in hand. They need to feel your enthusiasm and your passion. This is all about how you come across and the words and phrases that you use. But we'll look at this in more detail in Commandments 5, 7 and 8.

REMEMBER THEY'VE SEEN IT ALL BEFORE

Bankers, venture capitalists and private equity companies have to sift through literally hundreds of letters and phone calls from aspiring entrepreneurs. They probably sit through a hundred or so face-to-face pitches every year. So they've seen most of it all before. They will have bought into the ones that appealed to them on an emotional level and then they would have justified their decision with some logic. Things like, "It was the best, or a deal I just couldn't ignore." This book is about making sure that your pitch is one of those.

IN SHARON WRIGHT'S PITCH FOR INVESTMENT *(see over the page) she had demonstrated the credibility of the product and potential of the market. The Dragons wanted to know why she needed Dragons at all, and here Sharon appealed to them emotionally by saying that she needed help in some of the tricky business decisions she was having to negotiate – she wanted a business partner with experience by her side for guidance as well as investment. Carefully, she didn't say that she couldn't make the big decisions, merely that they took her a lot of time and anguish.*

" BELIEVE IN YOURSELF! HAVE FAITH IN YOUR ABILITIES! WITHOUT REASONABLE CONFIDENCE IN YOUR OWN POWERS YOU CANNOT BE SUCCESSFUL. "

NORMAN PEALE (1898–1993), AUTHOR OF 'THE POWER OF POSITIVE THINKING'

MAGNAMOLE

Sharon Wright gave as near to a perfect pitch as has ever been seen in the Den and it's instructive to break it down to see how she did so well. Firstly, she had a great product (see right) with obvious market potential. Secondly, it was a viable business – there was proven demand for the product and she was already selling it profitably.

FROM BEGINNING TO END, *Sharon's was an assured presentation, and her confidence came from tangible sources.*

Whilst demonstrating her product, Sharon explained the problem it solved and the cost savings benefits it offered. Not only was this last point a convincing argument in its own right, but it also showed that Sharon had carried out detailed market research. When you've invented a great device, it can be tempting to assume, or 'just know', that people will be queuing up to buy it; but, if you want investment, you need to prove the case.

Alongside the practicalities – patent in hand, contracts made with major companies etc – Sharon also dealt admirably with questions. Most required factual responses, but Peter's more challenging query about the limits to the business (once bought, there is no need to buy again), led to an expansive answer that indicated future related products.

Sharon's final triumph was to select the deal that suited her best. She had done her homework and knew which Dragons she most wanted to work with in order to make Magnamole a global product. So, while she could have left with exactly what she pitched for, she chose a higher offer of investment from Duncan and James and seized on the opportunity to negotiate a slightly better equity deal than they had offered.

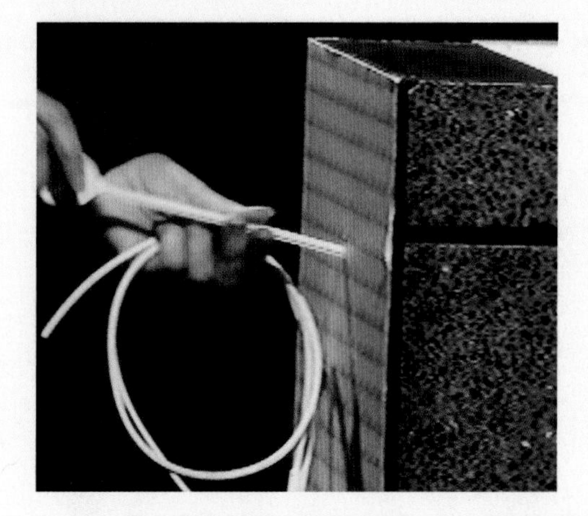

SHARON'S PRODUCT, MAGNAMOLE, *was a simple device for threading cabling through cavity walls, so she was able to demonstrate how it worked whilst talking the Dragons through the process. She explained why threading cable through walls was a problem, how her device provided a solution and why this could be of benefit to users – even to the point of giving figures for the savings in downtime usually spent by engineers trying to thread cable through walls using a coat hanger or drill bit.*

THE DRAGONS *were left with little negotiating power. It was more a case of which of the Dragons had most to offer.*

ULTIMATELY, *the deal with Duncan and James didn't come to fruition. Sharon did go on to get an even better offer, however, selling 10% of the company to a silent partner for £100,000.*

COMMANDMENT

KNOW THE AUDIENCE

What do you know about the people to whom you are speaking?

ONE OF THE MOST COMMON MISTAKES that pitchers make is to forget about who is in the audience. You must remind yourself that your audience is made up of individuals. Each one has a different personality and different hot buttons. So although a group of bankers might have a similar motivation, the way that each of them makes a decision will be slightly different. You can see this in action on every episode of Dragons' Den. Each Dragon is an individual character, reacting to a pitch in a different way to the other Dragons. What excites one might turn off another. Occasionally, the Dragons fight each other, and the clever pitcher can turn this to their advantage.

SCULPTOR GUY PORTELLI PROVED HIMSELF A QUICK THINKER IN THE DEN. *He was taken aback as offers came in from several Dragons. Theo was first to make him an offer. Peter then suggested that all five Dragons invest. Three were prepared to do this: James, Theo and Peter. Duncan put in a counter offer on his own, raising the level of investment from £70,000 to £90,000. Guy could have seen this as an either/or decision – they were both great offers after all. However, he took the opportunity to raise the level of investment from James, Theo and Peter to £80,000.* *Read his case study on pp54–5.*

Identifying your audience is about being a bit of an amateur psychologist. It may sound like a cliché, but you can actually work it all out from their job titles, their background, their body language and the questions they ask. Although we talked about how you are selling, in reality you are asking for their help. A stranger is unlikely to assist you just because you're a nice person. They need a reason and it has to be what they will get out of it.

One of Aesop's fables explains this beautifully. It tells the story of a peasant who took his axe to an apple tree that no longer bore fruit. After the first blow the birds who lived in its branches beseeched him not to cut it down. He asked them why he shouldn't, and they promised to sing to him every day. He shook his head and struck the tree again with his axe. The trunk split at the base and he saw that a swarm of bees lived there and it was full of honey. He stood back and put his axe away because he could eat the honey.

CASE STUDY **FROM SERIES 6 EPISODE 4**

RAPSTRAP

Andy Harsley's product, the Rapstrap, was a new kind of reusable cable tie. But creating a viable business from an invention – no matter how good – is never an easy or obvious path. Andy was well aware of this, and his pitch in the Den was very much about bringing on board the kind of investor who could help him take his product to market.

James and Duncan made him the offer, in exchange for a 50% equity stake. It was high, but Andy had gone to the Den to get a Dragon to fast-track his product to a wide market. With the offer, he had two Dragons and the opportunity to take the product beyond a national level, using the distribution chain that the Dragons were already using for other electrical products.

JAMES'S ARGUMENT, *justifying the 50% stake, was elegant and convincing: "Our objective is very simple, Andy. We want to make you a very successful entrepreneur."*

“THE BEST WAY TO PERSUADE PEOPLE IS BY LISTENING TO THEM ” DEAN RUSK, AMERICAN DIPLOMAT

Most people don’t take the time to understand the person they will deal with, let alone think about what drives them and what they want. Don’t confuse your own needs with theirs. Theirs will be different.

MOTIVATION OF THE GROUP

When you pitch to a group of similar people, whether they’re bankers, customers or the Dragons, everyone in the group will have a similar motivation. It is important that you understand this because it helps you get the emphasis of your pitch just right. You also need to make sure that you’ve targeted the group that is best for your needs. As you will see later, it’s no good talking to business angels unless you’re willing to let them get directly involved in your company. Similarly it’s no good meeting bankers if it’s a high-risk investment.

WHAT BANKERS ARE LOOKING FOR

- **SPECIALIST AREA.** The aims of each team of investment bankers is published, and you need to make sure that their objectives match what you’re after and what you’re willing to give. Some are high-yield funds; others specialize in technology companies or emerging markets. From this, you will have an idea of their primary motivation.

- **SAFETY AND REASSURANCE.** Bankers tend to be cautious. This is because they invest other peoples' money, often from pension funds. Therefore, generally bankers need to know their investment is safe – at least they want to get their money back. They want to know that you'll be able to pay the interest on the loan.

- **SOLID FACTS AND FIGURES.** You always need to give bankers lots of numbers and time to make their decision. They will look at your track record, what you offer as security and the detail in your financial projections.

WHAT VENTURE CAPITALISTS ARE LOOKING FOR

- **HIGH RETURNS WITHIN A FEW YEARS.** Venture capitalists and private equity companies look for much higher returns with an exit strategy or payout in three to five years time. They are looking for a percentage of your business and will take this in the form of debentures or shares.

- **POTENTIAL MARKET GROWTH.** Selling their stake is the exit strategy, either as a trade sale or flotation. Consequently they are more interested in the market and its potential growth than a banker would be.

" THERE ARE A LOT OF SO-CALLED EARLY STAGE VENTURE CAPITAL FIRMS THAT REALLY WANT THE ENTREPRENEUR TO PROVE THE VALIDATION AND HAVE ABOUT £1M OF REVENUE BEFORE THEY'LL GET INVOLVED. "

JULIE MEYER, ONLINE DRAGON

- **RETURN ON INVESTMENT (ROI).** The venture capitalists' self-interest is return on investment and you must convince them that you can exploit the market and successfully manage the growth of the company in the medium term.

- **BOARDROOM POWER.** They may also want to put one of their own on the board and get some experienced non-executive directors involved.

- **START-UPS AND MANAGEMENT BUYOUTS.** Venture capitalists will invest in start-ups (though see online Dragon Julie Meyer's view above) and management buyouts. With the latter their emphasis will change from market growth to your team's ability to exploit its current position in the market and cut costs. Their exit strategy, however, is always the same with a sale or flotation in three years.

CASE STUDY **FROM SERIES 5 EPISODE 9**

ABOUT TIME

Iain McGill and Joe Gill made a pitch in Series 5 for a board game called About Time. This general knowledge-based game focuses on time and dates.

Whilst the Dragons enjoyed a round of the game during the presentation, they were less enthusiastic about the projected figures. The duo anticipated incurring a debt of £80,000 in the first year and accruing a further debt of £25,000 in the second. Only in the third year did they forecast a year-end profit of £75,000. It was then that Peter Jones effectively pulled the plug on the pitch by suggesting that investing £50,000 in a business that isn't likely to make a profit for at least two years is a less than attractive proposition.

IAIN AND JOE *realized that they were not going to receive any money from the Dragons, but they didn't give up on their business idea.*

It may have been a case of no dice from the Dragons, but retailers did spot potential and Ian and Joe's game soon appeared in Hamleys. About Time is now stocked in high-street shops and has UK-wide distribution with Lakeland. Sales have expanded into the US market through Barnes & Noble and they have produced a German edition and a Guardian newspaper edition.

WHAT ANGEL INVESTORS ARE LOOKING FOR

- **PERSONAL INTEREST.** Business angels and other private investors are wealthy individuals who want to invest their money and possibly also their time in a business. They might be entrepreneurs themselves. Sometimes they are ex-managing directors of small- to medium-sized companies, who have taken early retirement or redundancy and a payout.

- **EQUITY.** Like venture capitalists, business angels want a share of your business – a percentage of shares to give them equity – but they would look at a much longer term exit strategy than venture capitalists would.

THE DIVISIONS BETWEEN INVESTORS ARE NOT ALWAYS CLEAR CUT, *and an investor may act as a business angel in one investment and as a venture capitalist in another. On the whole, Dragon Deborah Meaden (left) is more of a business angel. She likes to get involved in how a business runs and is prepared to retain a level of commitment over the long haul rather than for the two- to three-year returns.*

- **OPPORTUNITY FOR MENTORING.** Such investors love to invest in start-ups because they enjoy the warm glow from helping other entrepreneurs to succeed. Money may not be the biggest motivator for them. Yes, they want their investment to be secure, but it's the challenge of

JULIA CHARLES OF D4M – *an events company that featured in Series 6 – eventually bought back the share of equity she had ceded to Duncan and James in the Den. It was a personal decision for Julia: she simply wanted the business to be fully hers and not to have the added responsibility of making a profit for investors when making decisions about the direction of her business.*

being part of new businesses that excites them. That's their self-interest and you must emphasize the opportunity for them to be actively involved in your business.

- **INTERESTING IDEAS IN FAMILIAR MARKETS.** Such investors tend to be turned on by the product and may prefer to work in a market that they already understand.

TARGET THE RIGHT GROUP

The key issue for you is to decide which type of investor would best match your own situation, needs and way of working. Think about your ambition in terms of what you want to create. For example, do you want to build a dynasty which becomes yours and your children's

RONAN MCCARTHY'S SPIT 'N' POLISH SHOESHINE COMPANY *appeared in Series 7 and gives an example of expected levels of equity for investment at an early stage of a business. Ronan felt that his business would be 'low maintenance' from the Dragons' point of view and so they should require a relatively low percentage of equity. He was, however, asking for more than £100,000 and his business plan was yet to be tried and tested – he hadn't set up the first booth at the time of the pitch. The Dragons, therefore, considered it high risk, and so the only offer on the table was in exchange for a 40% stake in the business, which Ronan refused.*

business for the rest of your life? Or do you just want to make a pot of money in a relatively short period?

Business angels are valuable when you are looking at the longer term because they will bring a wealth of business experience. Whereas venture capitalists and private investors are usually looking for that pot of money in a three-year time-scale.

Imagine a road which has at one end just an idea for a business and at the other end a very successful established company. Think about where you are on this journey. An idea on its own is virtually worthless and you are probably the only person who's willing to invest time and money. An idea that has been developed into something, but doesn't yet have any customers, is high risk even if you have a wonderful business plan. Consequently an investor is going to want a very large stake so the potential reward will compensate them for the high chance of failure. For many investment bankers this risk is just too high. But a private investor or one of the Dragons might be interested.

Further along the road you have a small business that already has a few customers and therefore a proven product. The risk is lower and the business can probably generate the cash flow to exploit the market with the right amount of investment. This is the sort of business that would suit a business angel, venture capitalists and some investment bankers. More traditional high-street banks want low risk and security against any investment.

So be very clear about where you are and your ambitions. Be realistic about your goals and ensure that your figures are plausible and correctly value your company. Remember that the amount of equity you have to exchange for any investment will depend on the value that the investor places on your business multiplied by a probability factor.

Now that you've thought about the group as a whole you need to think about each individual in the team. You need to understand their role, their power and how they make decisions.

SHAUN PULFREY *didn't get investment for his Tangle Teezer hair brush when he went into the Den in Series 5, but he was ultimately happy with the way that things worked out. The needs and expectations of entrepreneurs vary, and while some seek the experience and business wisdom of the Dragons, others are happy to do things their own way and simply require the money to move forward. In Shaun's case, rather than giving away equity, he obtained a loan that he was able to repay the following year. Since then, the profits have provided funds for reinvestment in product development and growing the business.*

ROLE OF EACH INDIVIDUAL

When you have to pitch to a group of people, each one will have a slightly different role. Think about the example of a job interview. Often there will be two interviewers, one from human resources or personnel and the other your potential boss. The person from HR wants to check that you've told the truth on your CV and are qualified to do the job. Whereas your potential boss wants to know if you'll fit in and that the chemistry between you is right.

THE DRAGONS DON'T ACT AS A TEAM – *indeed they often compete with each other – but there are group dynamics at play. Each has their own area of expertise and will lead the charge, so to speak, when a business pitch lands in their territory – either to swoop for a deal or to take the entrepreneur to task. Dragons have even been known to step away from a deal, as did Peter and Deborah with Rapstrap (see p39), if they conclude that there are other Dragons better placed industry-wise to invest. All the Dragons are well-versed in the financial aspects of business, of course, and almost take it in turns to drill down into the finances of each business opportunity.*

It's the same with a pitch. One person in the audience will be the decision maker, another might be an expert on the market and someone else will want to dig deep into your financial projections. It's easy to find out which one's which from their job title and the sort of questions that they ask. You must be prepared for all three to be in the audience with lots of backup information on the market and on your financials. There will probably also be others, who may not even be in the room, who will go through your take-away pack in detail.

“ MONEY WAS NEVER A BIG MOTIVATION FOR ME, EXCEPT AS A WAY TO KEEP SCORE. THE REAL EXCITEMENT IS PLAYING THE GAME. ”

DONALD TRUMP, AMERICAN BUSINESS MAGNATE

POWER OF EACH INDIVIDUAL

Power can come from three places. It can come from **AUTHORITY**, such as the case with a boss. It can come from **INFLUENCE**, as in a case where an individual is respected within a group or has connections to other people who have authority. Finally, power can come from **KNOWLEDGE OR EXPERTISE**. An expert has the power to rubbish your idea or to veto it as unworkable.

You will recognize each individual's power by how the rest of the group treats them, by what sort of questions they ask and by which part of your pitch they get particularly interested in. Do not dismiss the experts by ignoring them, or by not giving them what they want. The expert has an amazing amount of power and respect. You ignore them at your peril.

HOW PEOPLE MAKE DECISIONS

A lot of work has been done over the last hundred years to try and measure people's personalities. These days psychometric tests are fairly accurate and very comprehensive. Whilst you might need a degree in psychology to interpret some of them, there are a few quick and easy ways to determine someone's personality at work. Salespeople instinctively use these models to accurately predict someone's decision-making style.

The models describe four traits that almost everybody has. Sometimes it's just one trait that drives their work character; other people might have two that are more prominent than the rest. They are known as decision-making styles and will help you determine the best way to sell your idea to all the different types of individuals in your audience. The difficulty arises when you have to pitch to a group of people with different personality styles. Then you have to mix the type of information that you give and how you deal with them.

- A **DECISIVE** person walks and talks fast and will often have a relatively short attention span. These people get bored easily and will make a decision very quickly, often because it just feels right. They're unlikely to change their minds and if you give them too much information they will switch off. They are interested in actions and outcomes, not the detail. So stick to business, tell them

DUNCAN BANNATYNE IS A VERY DECISIVE DRAGON. *He tends to make up his mind fast and is extremely unlikely to be swayed once he has done so. Even if he warms to an entrepreneur pitching for investment, that rapport is unlikely to be the prime motivating force in deciding whether or not to make an offer – there have to be sound factual reasons too.*

“TRULY SUCCESSFUL DECISION MAKING RELIES ON A BALANCE BETWEEN DELIBERATE AND INSTINCTIVE THINKING”

MALCOLM GLADWELL, AMERICAN AUTHOR

what you've done so far and what you're going to do next. They are driven by results, so you must tell them about your past achievements and the outcomes you're going to achieve in the next few months. Private investors are usually Decisive people, and so are the Dragons.

- The **ANALYTICAL** person loves detail and is high on planning, facts and logic. Such people tend to be very well organized, precise and think in a linear way. Risk adverse, they often hold jobs that involve numbers such as in finance. You can recognize them because they start to pay attention when you talk figures or show graphs. They need time to consider all the facts, and their decisions are deliberate so you can't rush them. You must give them all the data they need and justify what you say. Make sure that your numbers stack up and your take-away pack looks organized and professional.

- The **SCEPTICAL** person is exactly as described and often an expert. You will need to work hard and demonstrate to them that you have the knowledge and credibility. Try not to take offence by the way the Sceptics in your audience challenge your ideas and the data that you've used to support your business case.

ALL THE DRAGONS PLAY DEVIL'S ADVOCATE TO SOME DEGREE – *it goes with the territory when scrutinizing a business plan – and no one likes to test a business proposition more than Peter. He will often voice considerable doubt in the Den. However, he is often still weighing things up and can be persuaded by further argument or more information. Having expressed all his doubts, he may yet offer investment if he thinks the opportunity is sufficiently viable. Such was the case with Tech 21 (see pp204–5). Peter poured scorn on the entrepreneur's valuation of his business, but then offered a deal, using his scepticism as leverage for a substantial equity stake.*

" INVESTING IN A BUSINESS THAT DOESN'T MAKE MONEY FOR TWO OR THREE YEARS IS ABOUT AS ATTRACTIVE AS QUASIMODO "

PETER JONES, DRAGON

- The **FOLLOWER** is a 'people-person' who is warm, friendly and helpful. Followers tend to go along with what other people have done. Although they are usually bright and curious they feed off references and you should talk about your testimonials and the people who've recommended your idea to others. You will need to be patient with a Follower as they are infuriatingly slow in making a decision. Trust is important, so relax and don't try to chivvy, otherwise the Follower will start to distrust you because they think you're hiding something.

In summary of this Commandment – 'Know the Audience' – you can see that before you even think about your pitch you need to be very clear about what sort of investor you want for your business.

Is it just money you want? If so, you need a banker. The venture capitalists will be looking for growth and an exit in three years, but they take more risk. For a longer term view the business angel is ideal. They will bring expertise to grow your business into a sizeable and successful operation, in the medium to long term.

Other kinds of private investors may be like venture capitalists and also looking for money, but often with a good network of connections that you can use to build your business very fast.

When you've chosen the group that you want to target, you need to understand that each person you pitch to will have a different hot button, different role and different way of making a decision. Make sure that you play to each one of them to win.

GUY PORTELLI

It is often assumed that you have to begin a Den pitch by offering a low percentage of equity in return for investment, the reasoning being that the Dragons will always negotiate it up. Guy Portelli showed that this doesn't have to be the case, when he asked for £70,000 for 25% equity in the sale of an edition of 100 sculptures that he intended to exhibit at the Mall Galleries in London.

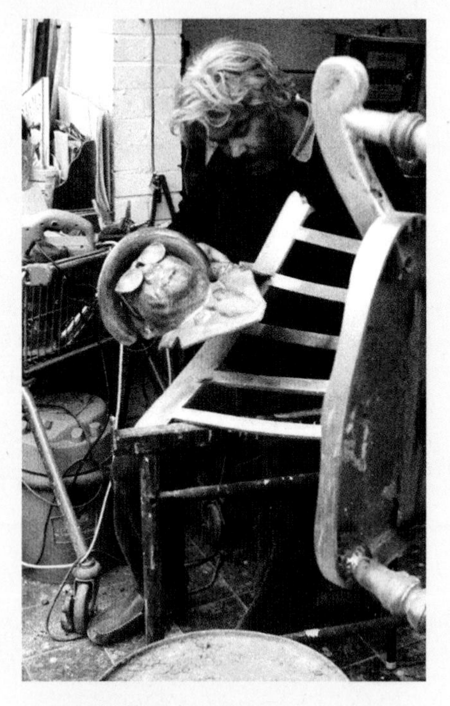

GUY WORKING IN HIS STUDIO *on a sculptural portrait of the iconic blues musician John Lee Hooker.*

Through examples of past sales and his projected figures for the future sales, Guy demonstrated that he was offering an appropriate level of equity for the amount of investment he was seeking – in fact, it appeared to be a very good deal for an investor. That being the case, the Dragons didn't try to whittle away at Guy's level of equity at all. In the end, Guy was able to negotiate himself an even better deal, by using Duncan's offer of an increased level of investment to persuade a consortium of Theo, Peter and James to agree to upping their offer to £80,000 for the 25% stake he had offered. This was the deal that was struck.

GUY'S SCULPTURE *of Miles Davis (right), with Tupac Shakur in the background, and (below) Guy with the Spice Girls portrait.*

HERE IS GUY'S OWN TAKE ON HOW TO APPROACH THE DEN. *"If you go in blindly optimistic that you can outsmart the Dragons, you will be standing in front of an audience of five million people eating humble pie, and it will look as if you don't respect the Dragons, or have no business acumen or you have just guessed at a figure. By calculating your best offer, which is one that gives both parties a reasonable piece of the cake, offering it and then being able to justify your calculation, you will at least keep your self respect, even if that's all you walk away with."*

COMMANDMENT 3

STRUCTURE YOUR PITCH

How can you make your points clearly?

YOU HAVE A VERY LIMITED TIME in which to make a pitch, therefore you have to structure the pitch carefully. It is perfectly possible to put across even very complex ideas in a matter of minutes. But the more concise you need to be, the more effort you need to put into planning your structure. No matter how clever and attentive the people in your audience are, they won't appreciate a presentation that starts meandering off the point or making the same point over and over. They might get confused or find you boring and irritating. And, of course, they might not be especially attentive in the first place… So, you need to know exactly where you're going with your presentation, and not allow any rambling.

By now you should have an idea of the shape of your presentation – a 'present with a ribbon' or a 'jigsaw' (see p29). Next you need to work on the structure and then research it to get all the facts and figures to support your case. As we said before, it will have three elements. We will recap what they are and then go into more detail:

1. **PRESENTATION.** If you are allowed to control the length of the presentation, we would suggest you aim for about 20 minutes. Ideally you will be speaking from head-notes and using a variety of props.

2. **QUESTION AND ANSWER SESSION.** You need to prepare for questions that are likely to be asked after you've given your presentation. Whilst you will never know exactly what they might ask, you can anticipate many questions. You should prepare a sheet of answers in advance – obviously this document will be for your own use only.

3. **TAKE-AWAY PACK.** Include all the background information on market size, sales projections and financials that your audience can take with them after the presentation. It's useful if you can memorize which page has what piece of information on it.

Every good pitch needs a strong argument and a structure that your audience will recognize. This will probably be the **PROBLEM-SOLUTION-ACTION** approach we talked about in Commandment 1, and which we will be reiterating in some of the examples of this

BLINDS IN A BOX, *which featured in Series 6, was a 'problem-solution-action' story for one of the company's founders, Simeone Salik. Having moved into a new home, she had wanted some breathing space before deciding on all the interior fabrics, such as the curtains. As a stop gap, she wanted some inexpensive temporary blinds, but couldn't find any in the UK. A problem for one person doesn't imply a ready market, but Simeone was sure that her problem was not unique and was convinced that there was potential for such a product. James Caan and Duncan Bannatyne agreed, and invested in the business. The blinds have indeed found a ready market and are now sold widely throughout the UK and distributed in Spain, France, Australia and New Zealand.*

chapter. If you have a clear structure, you'll come across as confident and not start rambling. You must finalize your structure before writing notes about the actual speech. To do that you must put pen to paper and start to think about the content of your pitch and the way your audience is going to take it in.

HOW PEOPLE TAKE IN INFORMATION

There is an important point you need to think about before you start, which is the fact that people absorb information in different ways through the senses. Although we all see, hear, touch, taste and smell, psychologists have discovered that each of us prefers one particular sense over another. We depend on this preferred sense to gather data from around us and understand the world.

PROWASTE *(see opposite), after obtaining £200,000 of investment from Duncan and Deborah, relocated from Surrey to London to be closer to its main customer base. The company is currently providing recycling solutions for major construction projects in the capital. Prowaste was also awarded Construction Recycler of The Year in 2009 at the National Recycling Awards.*

For example, you might be one of the 50% of people who prefer pictures over sounds. Your memory will consist mainly of images, and when you see something new you will subconsciously compare it with the images stored in your head. In that case your preferred mode of communication is visual. In other words, you trust your eyes rather than your ears or feelings. You will say things like, "Looks good to me" or "I see what you mean" and "I get the picture". If you go and buy a new car, you will be excited about its shape and colour rather than the sound of the engine. You are known as a Visual person.

However if you prefer sounds over pictures you are one of the 20% of people who are auditory. Musicians, professional speakers and radio presenters obviously have an affinity with sounds and trust their ears over their eyes or feelings. If you are like them, you will say things like, "Tell me more" or "Sounds good to me" and "I hear what you're saying". You probably like soothing background noise when you work and are irritated by loud interruptions. You may have a pleasant and dynamic voice and also tend to talk to yourself. When

CASE STUDY **FROM SERIES 6 EPISODE 8**

PROWASTE

Prowaste Management Services is a perfect case of a problem-solving business. Company director Paul Tinton made a pitch in the Den in 2008, when he explained that, under legislation that came into force that year, construction companies working on projects worth more than £300,000 had to prepare a site waste management plan before beginning work.

Realizing that this would be a big headache for the construction companies, Prowaste decided not just to be commercial waste recyclers but to provide a service that dealt with the whole caboodle. They would provide a full Site Waste Management Programme (SWMP) for clients, ensuring that as much site waste as possible was recycled and that the entire operation conformed to the latest legislative requirements. So while there were other waste and recycling companies in the market, none was dealing with the matter as comprehensively, giving Prowaste a unique market presence. It was a well-articulated pitch and attracted the investment of Duncan and Deborah.

PAUL TINTON *offered a problem-solving solution to waste management.*

IF POSSIBLE, LET YOUR AUDIENCE TOUCH *your product sample, which will especially appeal to any Kinaesthetic people present. Even a prosaic product such as DDN's device for preventing the misfuelling of vehicles (see pp226–7) can become more appealing if it can be touched and examined.*

you have to make a decision you probably run things through in your head over and over again. If you go to buy a car you'll be more interested in the sound system, the clunk of the door closing and the noise of the engine. If that's the case you are known as an Auditory person.

Alternatively you might be one of the 30% of people who trust their feelings over what they see or hear. You will be very tactile and highly tuned into your own and other people's emotions. You will use phrases like "I get what you're telling me" or "That feels good to me" and "Fill me in on what you're doing". You might pause a lot when you talk, so you can check out the other person's feelings and keep in touch with what's going on around you. You will probably be a good negotiator who can tune into other people but you might find it difficult to reason logically. If that's you, you are known as a Kinaesthetic.

Don't bother trying to identify and buttonhole the members of your audience into the three groups. Although we all have a preferred style of taking in information, it's not necessarily our only way of communicating. We use the other senses to a lesser degree and this might change according to our environment – you could be a Visual at work but a Kinaesthetic at home. In fact most people favour two styles over the third. What you have to do in your pitch is cover all three modes so you can connect with all the people that are likely to be in your audience.

Think images, words and feelings.

- **APPEALING TO THE VISUAL PEOPLE.** Visuals like pictures, graphs and charts. On average, half your audience will respond to this sort of visual information. They will quickly take on board the images that the rest of the audience might find more difficult. These days we are used to high-quality graphics on television, so your visuals must look professional. No fancy colours, no bells and whistles, though, just clear and simple. All your charts and graphs must be unambiguous so everyone can get the message whatever their preferred style.

- **APPEALING TO THE AUDITORY PEOPLE.** Auditories prefer sounds, so your words and phrases are very important. You must take time to tell the audience what each of your images, charts and graphs is actually saying. Also, anecdotes, stories and quotations will appeal to them. See also Commandment 7 about the voice.

- **APPEALING TO THE KINAESTHETIC PEOPLE.** Kinaesthetics like to touch and feel things. So you need to use props and hand out samples of your product. See Commandment 5 about props.

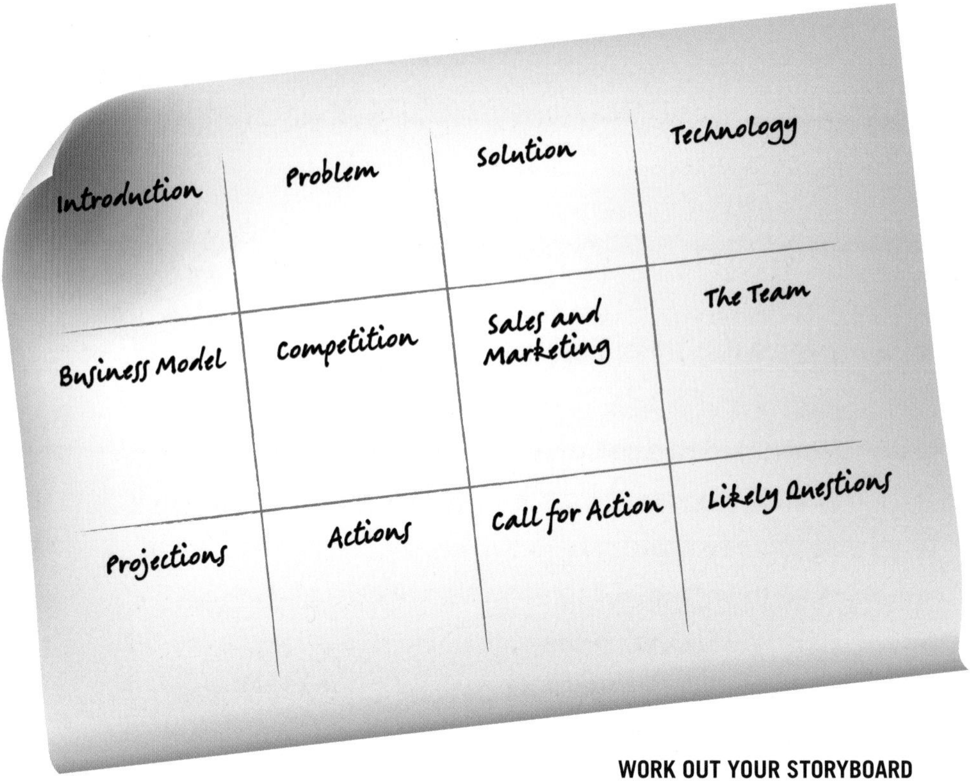

WORK OUT YOUR STORYBOARD
on a large piece of paper in landscape format.

STORYBOARD YOUR STRUCTURE

Make some space and time to be creative. It's quite difficult to do this in your own office because you'll easily get distracted. One of the best ways is to go away for a few days. Not too far, but somewhere relaxing where you won't be disturbed. You need to develop a very clear idea of what you're trying to achieve and brainstorm the essence of what you're going to say.

When you're settled get yourself a large sheet of plain A2 paper or a flip-chart sheet folded in half. Place it on a table in landscape format and divide it into twelve boxes by drawing two horizontal lines and three vertical ones. What you're going to do is create a storyboard for your pitch, a bit like storyboarding for a film or TV show. Each box is a topic in your presentation.

- **INTRODUCTION.** The first box, say the top left, is where you put down your thoughts on the introduction. How are you going to start your pitch? It is usual to introduce yourself, thank them for seeing you and explain the structure of your presentation. Don't tell them too much at this point. Remember it's rather like unwrapping a present or building up a picture in a jigsaw (see p29). You're either going to say, "I'm looking for an investment of £xxx," which is the present with the ribbon approach. Or, "I have a winning idea and an amazing opportunity for you." That's the jigsaw approach.

In the next 10 boxes you should jot down your thoughts about each of the topics in the list that follows. The reason you have 10 topics is that research has shown that these days most people can't cope with any more than about 10 different concepts at a time.

1 **PROBLEM.** Describe the problem that your idea solves, outline a typical customer and estimate the size and growth of the market. Make a list of all the information you already have and jot down what else you need to research on a separate sheet of paper. In the 1970s James Dyson's problem was that dust in his Hoover vacuum cleaner kept clogging the bag. So he designed a vacuum cleaner that didn't lose suction.

TOBY AND OLIVER RICHMOND'S BUSINESS, *Servicing Stop, featured in Series 7. This agency for servicing vehicles across the UK was growing rapidly and the brothers wanted to make the most of the market conditions. In an economic downturn, people look for cheaper options, and their service was better value than the car dealerships with whom they were competing. In their pitch they gave a clear vision for growth. Their service was good value and efficient, so customers were happy to use them, but they were a young company and, to be a national player, needed to get their name out there and make their brand as visible in the market as possible. To this end, they were already spending £30,000 on advertising per month. The investment they sought was specifically to inject even more impetus into marketing in order to take a greater stake of the market.*

2 **SOLUTION.** Introduce your idea or product and explain why people would buy it. James Dyson's vacuum cleaner didn't have a bag which meant that it didn't get clogged up and lose suction. At this point in your presentation you should plan to hand out samples of your product or something tangible to do with your idea. You want them to touch and play with what you're passionate about.

3 **TECHNOLOGY.** Describe the underlying technology of your idea or product and what's magical about it. You must get them excited and explain what makes it different from everything else out there. The Dyson vacuum

“ I MADE SOME MONEY IN THE COMMERCIAL PROPERTY BOOM AND KEPT GOING FROM THERE, ALWAYS LOOKING FOR THE RIGHT DEAL, THE RIGHT OPPORTUNITY. I LEARNED FOCUS, HARD WORK AND, MOST OF ALL, TO IDENTIFY AND KNOW MY MARKET. ” THEO PAPHITIS, DRAGON

cleaner used a unique cyclone technology that made it totally different from anything else on the market. It also made it look and sound different.

4 **BUSINESS MODEL.** Explain how you are going to make money – the pricing structure and gross margin.

5 **COMPETITION.** Talk about the competition in general terms and market shares. Describe the two market leaders in detail and how you stack up against them.

6 **SALES AND MARKETING.** Describe how you intend to sell and market your product. Explain what you have already achieved and outline your sales and marketing plan for the next 12 months.

7 **THE TEAM.** Describe the background of the key people in your business and include their CVs in the take-away pack. Outline the type of people you need to recruit over the next 12 months.

8 **PROJECTIONS.** This is where you present your sales forecasts and financials with detailed time scales.

9 **ACTIONS.** Summarize what you have already achieved and what actions and activities you have planned over the next few months.

10 **CALL FOR ACTION.** Use attention-grabbing words to describe the market opportunity in financial terms. Explain what you're looking for in terms of investment.

The final box is for jotting down the sorts of questions that you think they will ask, but you may not be able to think of many questions at the moment, in which case just leave it blank for now.

Now you need to stand back and run through your full storyboard in your head. When you've done this, ask yourself the following questions about the storyboard:

- **DOES IT FLOW LOGICALLY** from one box to the next? If not, you may have to think about how you link it from one topic to the next. Or you might have to reorder it slightly. Remember we talked about how it should unfold slowly.

- **DOES IT HAVE A COMPELLING ARGUMENT** and clearly explain the opportunity? If you are unsure, go through it with a friend – ideally one who doesn't know anything about the market.

- **DOES IT DEMONSTRATE YOUR EXPERTISE?** Your knowledge must be put across in the structure and content of your presentation.

- **DO YOU HAVE ENOUGH FACTS AND FIGURES** to make a credible take-away pack? This is an essential part of your pitch, and the people will go through it with a fine-tooth comb and pass it to their experts for checking. Note down what else you think you need on a separate sheet of paper. You can research the information and re-run your spread-sheets later.

YOU MIGHT BE FORGIVEN *for thinking that people putting the wrong fuel in their cars couldn't be that much of a problem, but in Michael Cotton's pitch for DDN (see pp226–7) he made the Dragons sit up and take notice at the facts and figures involved. Using industry figures, Michael declared that misfuelling cars happens at least 150,000 times a year in the UK. This convincingly made the case that the problem was a credible one. He went on to explain that DDN's patented device was the only such product that retrofits onto existing diesel vehicles, thereby demonstrating that they had a very good solution to the problem. Finally, he stated that there are 11 million diesel vehicles in the UK and 78 million in Europe, giving an idea of the market potential for the product.*

- What is the **ONE MESSAGE** that the audience will take away from your presentation? It's quite difficult to answer this question objectively when you are the one that's written it. So ask your friend.

IN THE CONFUSION OF ROB AND GEOFF'S LADDERBOX PITCH *(see opposite), and through the Dragons' need to constantly re-state questions in order to get a clear response, Rob lost track of his figures and began to sound vague and unsure of himself.*

By now, you will probably have identified a number of questions that are likely to be asked during the pitch, which you can write in the twelfth box. Include the questions that your friend asked.

WORK ON YOUR CONTENT

Before you start to write the actual content of your presentation it's best to sleep on it for a couple of days to allow your brain to work on it subconsciously. Then you can jot down any other thoughts that you might have. After those couple of days you need to get into a quiet place again and prepare the words that you're going to use. You shouldn't have to write a script, because what you say will be coming from your heart.

- **USE HEAD-NOTES.** The best way to work on your content is to write head-notes that will stimulate your brain to say the words. What you must do is devise your 'train of thought' because you'll be able to remember that. However, you might want to script and learn the opening because it sets the scene for your presentation and when you first stand up you'll be nervous.

CASE STUDY **FROM SERIES 6 EPISODE 6**

LADDERBOX

Father and son Geoff and Rob Hill went into the Den in Series 6, seeking investment in Ladderbox, a tool box and a lidded paint and roller system that fits all types of ladders.

Though a down-to-earth and functional product, the pitch soon veered away from common sense as the duo lost focus and began interrupting and talking over the top of one another. It made for a lively and comical pitch, but the comedy then reflected on the product, which lost credibility as a result. On the day, Rob and Geoff gave the impression that they might not be taking the business as seriously as they might.

THE LADDERBOX *tool system in action.*

As Rob admits, "If we had got investment with a Dragon with their proven record of getting products rapidly to market, things would have moved quicker, but we got there on our own in the end, after gaining investment in the tooling and signing a three-year worldwide licensing deal... We do take our business seriously, but we have a very fun and unique business style and work very well with our committed team."

- **INCLUDE EXAMPLES AND ANALOGIES.** As you put together your head-notes, think about examples and analogies, rather than just dry facts. Tell them some 'war stories' (see p88) and anecdotes about the challenges that you've had to overcome and your achievements so far. Remember they want to see that you have the determination and stamina to deliver results.

- **RECORD YOURSELF.** When you've finished making your head-notes, take a recording device and say your presentation out loud. When you've finished it, sit back and listen objectively to the recording. Ask yourself the five questions that you went through before. You should also now have some sort of idea how long your talk will last – 20 minutes is ideal, remember.

- **KEEP PRACTISING.** Make any changes to your head-notes and record yourself speaking out loud several more times. When you reach the point that you're reasonably happy, listen to your last recording and ask yourself this question – does it whet the appetite before you go for the kill and ask for their support? If it doesn't, you need to go back and change the structure and your head-notes and do it all over again (maybe in another session). If it does, then you need to move on and get together all the facts and figures you will need to put in the take-away pack. (You'll be rehearsing again when you've worked on your props, voice and body language.)

THE FIVE CS FOR A PERFECT PITCH

Five things will make your pitch successful. The structure of your presentation contributes to the first two – clarity and confidence. A clear structure will stop you from rambling and will show the audience that you're confident in yourself. When you know what you're doing and where your presentation is going you can easily respond to someone who asks a question when you're in full flight and still return to your argument.

- **CLARITY** of purpose and clear and concise content.
- **CONFIDENCE** in yourself and your idea.
- **CREDIBILITY** by demonstrating your knowledge and building trust (see the next Commandment).
- **CHUNKING** through bite-sized pieces that the audience can instantly take on board (see pp108–10).
- **CONNECTION** with the audience by understanding their motivation and responding to their questions.

The key to the soft seduction or soft-sell approach that we talked about earlier is the ability to put yourself in the audience's situation and decide what they want. Usually it's to do with money, power or status. In the context of your pitch it's probably a combination of money and status. Money is tangible and fairly easy to recognize; status is more difficult to understand. It comes from whether you can deliver what you promise. If they pick a winner their status and standing grows. If you fail, they take a hit both on their pockets and their status.

CASE STUDY **FROM SERIES 7 EPISODE 2**

THE WHOLELEAF COMPANY

Although he didn't receive any investment from the Dragons, Adejare Doherty gave a spirited and clearly focused pitch in the Den. It was an assured performance, in which he firstly outlined the nature of the company: to import, supply and distribute environmentally friendly disposable tableware made from Areca palm fronds.

ADEJARE BROUGHT A PALM LEAF *into the Den to show the Dragons the raw material and explain the process that turns the leaf into a plate; it helped visualize the process.*

The product's USP was that it was the only truly eco-friendly alternative to disposable paper plates. In explaining how and why this was the case, Adejare confidently set out the credentials of his business. The pitch quickly moved on to hard facts when Adejare revealed that Sainsbury's was trialling a picnic set in some of their stores. Selling into a major supermarket is obviously good if you want to sell in volume; the problem was that Adejare wasn't making any money on the deal. He revealed that the price at which he was selling them to Sainsbury's was the same as the cost of making, importing and distributing them: zero profit. Adejare quickly went on to explain that once able to buy in larger quantities, his costs would reduce to about 50%, allowing for a profit. Unfortunately, the quantities needed to reduce costs to this level were vast: over 10 million units. In an economic climate in which consumers were turning back to price over ethics, the Dragons couldn't foresee him selling enough to make the business investable.

Price became the insurmountable stumbling block in the pitch. The Dragons were convinced that not enough consumers would buy a premium-priced product. Adejare was equally convinced that it wouldn't be a premium-priced product if he could buy in large enough quantities.

Ultimately, they thought his projected figures were overly optimistic and that it was too great an investment risk – despite all agreeing that the product was excellent.

THE DRAGONS ALL AGREED *that the product was excellent, but they couldn't be persuaded that the interest from supermarkets and catering suppliers was sufficient to make it an investable business.*

THE WHOLELEAF COMPANY *has since negotiated better credit terms with their suppliers, which means that they do not need huge amounts of capital to buy stock. They are also now working with distributors, notably Remmerco (distributor of upscale packaging) and Pronto Pack, which supplies to outdoor festivals such as Glastonbury.*

COMMANDMENT 4

KNOW YOUR STUFF

Do you have a clear grasp of the facts and figures?

CREDIBILITY is a crucial element that will make your pitch successful. This is a combination of your knowledge and the amount of trust that the audience has in your ability to deliver results. Watch any episode of Dragons' Den and you will soon see how credibility is built up or falls apart on the basis of the apparent knowledge and trust-worthiness of the pitchers. Trust is about the confidence you have in yourself and your track record. So in this Commandment we show you how to ooze confidence without looking dangerously arrogant – this will boost your credibility during the pitch. That means you will have to ditch the lectern and script, and memorize your key facts and figures.

The participants on Dragons' Den can receive scathing comments if their credibility falls apart during their pitch.

"I DIDN'T LIKE THE PRESENTATION. I DON'T LIKE THE PRODUCT. AND I DON'T LIKE YOU, SO I'M OUT."

DUNCAN BANNATYNE, DRAGON

You obviously want to avoid this reaction (whether it's spoken or unspoken) from your audience. Instead, you will demonstrate knowledge and confidence from how you do your presentation, the way in which you answer questions and the information in the take-away pack that you hand out at the end. Your track record comes from your CV, your reputation and how you convince them that you will deliver what you promise.

DON'T PROJECT THE WRONG IMAGE WITH A LECTURE

Many people think that you need to write a full-blown script for a presentation in order to get it right. Nothing could be further from the truth. If you know your subject well enough, you'll come across as a confident and knowledgeable person. This is a pitch, not a lecture to be delivered behind a lectern.

IMAGE OF THE LECTERN

Imagine if you walk into the room with a thick sheath of papers and put them on a lectern. What would the audience think? They probably would groan and think, "Not another boring talk." They'll have sat through many similar presentations many times and will have become conditioned to thinking that you're about to deliver another mind-numbing one. The lectern is linked to politicians spouting vague promises, professors giving boring lectures and members of the clergy giving sermons in church.

The lectern is also a barrier that separates you from the audience. It looks as though you want to distance yourself from them and sends a very clear message that you don't have much confidence in yourself. You also look rigid, formal and lifeless because you're fixed to a single spot. And that's not something you want.

The audience will get a similar impression if you stand in front of them with the papers in your hands and start to read from a script.

The real message you want to send is: "I'm confident in what I'm going to talk about, so I don't need a script or notes." Therefore, if there's a lectern at the front of the room, move it to one side. If there's a table, stand in front of it, not behind it. Make sure that there are no barriers between yourself and the audience. You must connect with your audience and act as though you're having a conversation with them, rather than talking at them or giving them a lecture.

AFTER HAMFATTER'S PERFORMANCE AND NO-NONSENSE PITCH *(see right), they received interest from three of the Dragons. Duncan offered the money for 50% of everything (sales of past and future recordings plus live shows) until he had recouped his £75,000; thenceforth he would reduce his take to 10%. Peter offered a simple 30% stake for the money. Theo and Deborah combined forces to offer a similar deal to Duncan, but reducing to only 20% after recouping the investment money; their argument was that they could bring more to the table in terms of relevant experience and contacts. Hamfatter chose Peter's offer. They had done their homework about the relative merits of the potential investors and knew that Peter's music business contacts would make him the right choice for them.*

THE WRITTEN AND SPOKEN WORD

Hopefully, that's made you ditch any idea of reading straight from a script. Now this doesn't mean that you have to learn your script parrot-fashion. In fact, if anything, that's almost worse than using notes. You'll come across as stilted, with very little passion, enthusiasm or confidence.

We've become used to seeing presenters on television speaking straight to the camera without any obvious notes. When we think about it, we know that they're cheating because there's almost

HAMFATTER

Hamfatter is an indie pop band, which made for an unusual pitch on Dragons' Den. It consisted of the band playing part of one song – their biggest hit to date – then breaking down their modest successes so far and the figures for potential growth with their new album.

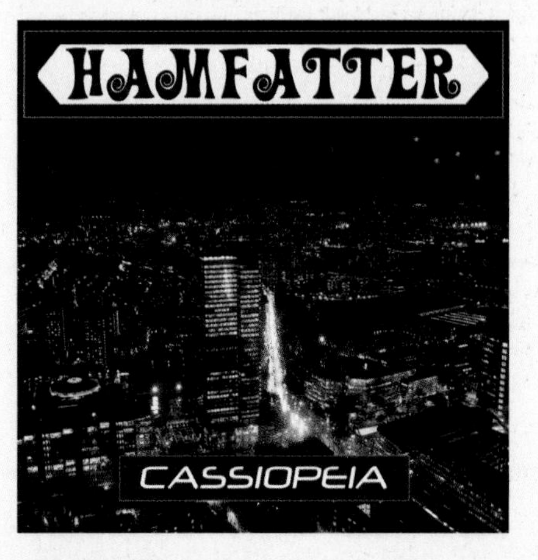

HAMFATTER'S *album 'Cassiopeia'.*

It was a surprisingly businesslike pitch for a music band, and they were clearly au fait with the numbers and the role that a marketing budget can play in levels of success. In the music business, there's a fine line between a hit and a miss, and sensibly Hamfatter chose to ask for a relatively small amount of money. This made the prospect of investment all the more worthwhile, and they attracted three offers from Duncan, Peter, and from Theo and Deborah jointly. It was a tough choice to make on the spot, but the musicians plumped for Peter's experience in the music industry.

Since the Den, Hamfatter have released the album 'Cassiopeia', some of which was recorded with top producer Joe Chicarelli, plus a solo album by lead singer Eoin O'Mahony.

ALL OF THE ENTREPRENEURS *who make it to the Den are well prepared. Knowing the extra level of intensity in the Den, most take preparations very seriously. As* **CAROLYN JARVIS OF BUGGYBOOT** *said, "We were so well prepared. We had practised and practised. We practised in front of our friends … in front of our accountants." It showed, and she and partner Charlotte Evans made an assured pitch for their business in Series 6, eventually securing investment from Deborah Meaden.*

KAREN O'NEILL AND KAREN COOMBES *of KCO* *(see also p182)* *made a theatrical pitch, including speaking in unison at certain points during the presentation: "We practised our pitch every time we called each other; whenever we saw new people we'd get ourselves a little audience, then we'd practise it together. We were really chuffed with ourselves – everything went according to plan – until they started asking questions…" Practising your own part is only half the battle. You also need to anticipate what you'll be asked and practise responding to those questions too.*

certainly an auto-cue or some kind of teleprompt with the words scrolling just above the camera lens. But subconsciously you might think that, because the television presenters sound so natural, they're not using a script and they know what they're talking about.

What is not so apparent is that the television presenters will have rehearsed with the auto-cue, and the script will have been written by a professional who understands the difference between the written and spoken word.

The **WRITTEN WORD** is designed to be taken in at your leisure. The reader has time to go back and check when they didn't understand the previous passage. What will happen if you write a script is that you'll read and re-read it to yourself, editing and tweaking it until you feel its right. But however pleased you feel about the final result, it will sound canned because you're not used to reading out aloud.

By contrast, the **SPOKEN WORD** is spontaneous and comes from the heart. The listener doesn't just hear the words, there's the tone and pace of your voice, and the emphasis you put on the important phrases. The spoken word doesn't exist without a speaker, and it's their enthusiasm and their voice that brings it to life. When you talk from the heart it becomes a performance. But when you read a written speech out loud it will seem controlled and manipulative. Later, in Commandment 7, we look at how you can improve your voice to put passion into the words you say.

- **RESPONSIVE SPEAKERS.** A good speaker will vary the way they speak and the words they use in response to the reaction of the audience. They will skip over the parts which don't seem to interest the audience and spend longer on the bits that excite them.

- **PROBLEM OF THE WRITTEN SPEECH.** With the written speech you don't have the flexibility to be responsive. If you stray off the script, you'll struggle to find your way back to your place and will end up feeling like an amateur.

- **PROBLEM OF THE UNSTRUCTURED SPEECH.** You probably know what you want to say, but on the day your nerves may dull your memory. So even though you know your idea or product backwards, you will waffle unless you have a very clear structure or train of thought. Without it you will ramble, wander and meander to such an extent that the audience will lose track, feel confused and be unimpressed.

MICHAEL PRITCHARD DEMONSTRATED *the Anyway Spray in Series 7 (see also p123). For this special household spray that can work upside down and any other position you choose to use it, he explained the technology that had gone into it in simple terms: "A conventional dip tube has got one hole in it and an Anyway tube has got about a billion. And the Anyway tube prefers liquids to gases, so liquids go through, gases don't." It gave a succinct impression of the technology rather than a full explanation – enough to convey why this spray was better than a conventional one.*

THE SOLUTION

What you need are notes. Not that you'll use notes on the day – that would send the wrong signal. Don't worry, you won't have to learn your presentation by heart. But you will need to remember your train of thought, which is the structure of your presentation. By rehearsing and repeating your speech again and again you can memorize your notes so you are comfortable with the flow of your presentation. If you're worried that you might forget something, put your notes in your pocket in case of an emergency. Even professional speakers do that.

If you spend enough time on rehearsals, you'll be able to interrupt your flow or even divert to answer a burning question and come back to where you left off. Then your confidence will stand out, which will reinforce your credibility.

THE POWER OF THREE

You already have an overall structure for your presentation on your storyboard with its 10 topics. Now you must work out the structure for each of those topics and create notes that will become your train of thought in such a way that they stimulate your brain to remember the words at the right time.

THE SECRET TO KNOWING WHERE YOU'RE GOING AND WHAT YOU'RE GOING TO SAY IS SIMPLE – THINK IN THREES

The brain finds it very easy to remember a sequence of three things. If you ask someone to name three fizzy soft drinks they will quickly come up with Coke, Pepsi and one other. Then they'll have to stop and think. It's the same if you ask them to name mobile phones and any other type of product. The 'Power of Three' is why you keep seeing or hearing the same advert over and over again. Advertisers need to constantly push their brand so it's one of the three stuck in your head.

You can apply the Power of Three to the overall structure of your presentation. Think of it as three sections:

- **PROBLEM**
- **SOLUTION**
- **ACTION**

IN RED BUTTON DESIGN'S PITCH *in Series 5, the young duo firstly explained the problem they were addressing – a shortage of available clean water in disaster zones in the developing world – and then talked the Dragons through the technical solution they had devised, which would be targeted at aid agencies. Now called the Midomo, this is a water-carrying vessel that a person can push along. The clever technological bit is that, as the wheels turn, they power a filtration apparatus that cleans the water in transit. The Dragons were impressed by the ingenuity of their design, creating a single product for water storage, transportation and filtration.*

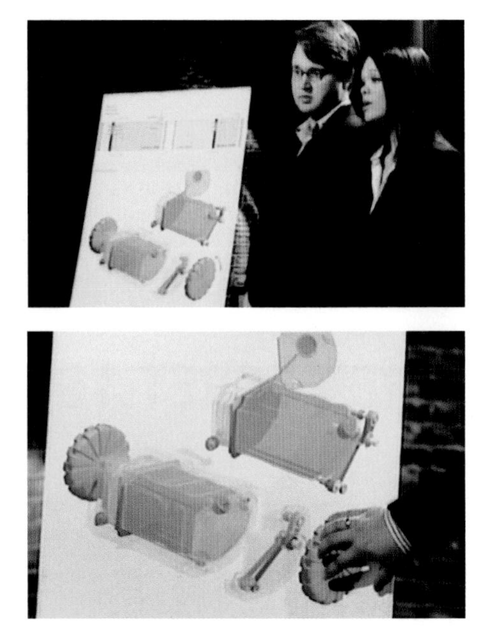

You can then further subdivide those sections into threes. For example, the Problem part can have three topics:

- **BACKGROUND TO THE PROBLEM**
- **THE PROBLEM ITSELF**
- **WHAT THE PROBLEM MEANS TO PEOPLE**

Likewise, the Solution part can have three topics:

- **WHAT MY SOLUTION IS**
- **WHY PEOPLE WOULD BUY IT**
- **THE MAGICAL TECHNOLOGY IT USES**

Now we naturally tend to write notes with long phrases because we think we'll forget. But in fact the opposite is true. It's much easier to remember single words or very short phrases that stimulate your thought processes so you automatically say the right words. Therefore, all you might need as a mental prompt for the Solution part of your presentation is three words:

- **WHAT**
- **WHY**
- **MAGIC**

You need to rehearse and rehearse until all this stuff's in your head. The best way to do this is standing up because that's how you're going to give your pitch in the end. Put your tape recorder on the table, stand with your head notes in your hand and give your pitch, mentally prompting yourself in threes wherever possible.

Play back your recording and check your head notes if necessary. Repeat the process until you are reasonably happy. Then do it without notes, but still thinking in threes, and see how you get on.

You'll probably be surprised, but words should soon seem to flow automatically from your head, with the mental 'threes' providing all the simple prompts and mental checks you need.

SHOW THEM YOU CAN DELIVER

One of the best ways to prove to your audience that you have a track record of achievement is to use stories to capture their imagination. These add a human side to all the dry facts and allow you to show off your passion and determination. They build trust and reinforce the message that you will deliver on what you promise.

A useful approach is to think of your story as a war analogy – a description of your triumph in the face of adversity. The 'war story' should be about a minute long and describe a problem you recently came across, what you did and the result.

The Power of Three applies here, too, so the 'war story' is:

- **PROBLEM**
- **ACTION**
- **RESULT**

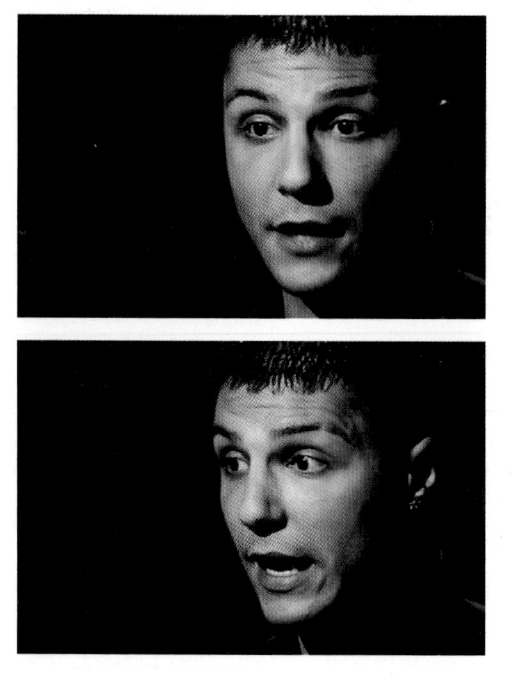

IN TONY EARNSHAW'S PITCH *for UK Commercial Cleaning in Series 7, he was asked by the Dragons to tell them about his background. He told a classic tale of ambition and endeavour: how he had started out "from nothing", as he put it, and through his actions – "hard graft" – had built up a window cleaning round into a very profitable small business. How, not content with that, he had set his sights on the commercial sector and started a new business for that purpose, winning major contracts and resulting in a yet more profitable business. His next step was to make it the biggest and best company of its kind in the UK. It's a story that would have struck a chord with the Dragons, and Duncan in particular seemed to warm to Tony's presentation.*

IN PETER NEATH AND IAN WORTON'S PITCH *for the Grillstream (see pp118–19), the duo successfully demonstrated that they had found a good solution to the problem of fat dripping through a grill during cooking. Unfortunately they didn't convince the Dragons that they knew how to take the product further and turn it into a profitable business.*

For example, the story could be something like, "Last year we had a problem with the generator as it kept failing after a couple of months. I brought in a new designer who worked up three alternatives which we bench-tested and put into the field. The one I finally chose was not only more efficient than the original design but is still operating 18 months later."

Write down some 'war stories' (why not make it three of them?) and give each one a label that you will remember. The label needs to conjure up the story in your mind, so you could use words like 'Quality Issue' or 'Bad Sample' or 'Beating off the Competition' – the more warlike the label the better (without going over the top).

WORK DOWN THE PYRAMID

As mentioned before, your presentation should be no longer than 20 minutes. Therefore, you must make sure that you don't overload it with too much information. Particularly as the Decisive people in the audience will switch off if you just tell them too much. Think in bite-sized chunks and start with a big picture working down to the detail. Newspapers and the news on television are organized just like a pyramid. The headline and the opening paragraph are the tip of the pyramid and make the main point of the story. You then move down the pyramid with more detailed information until you've got enough.

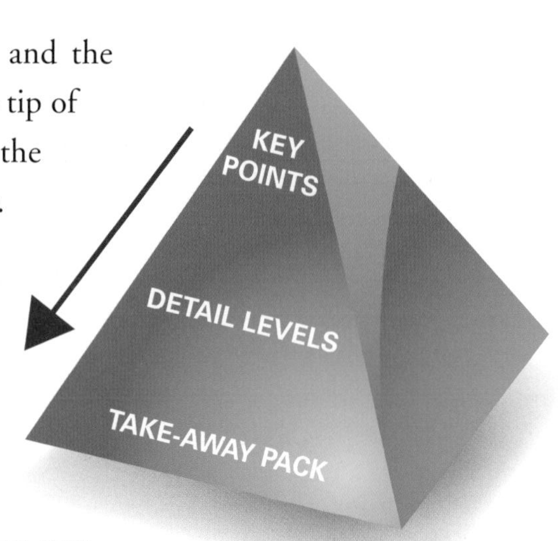

It's the same with your presentation. The knack is to decide where you start on the pyramid and how far to go down. It's the audience that tells you that. You know when eyes glaze over or they start to fidget, that they've had enough. And that's another reason for not using a script. You can easily move on to the next topic.

All the details behind your pitch, in other words the base of the pyramid, are in the take-away pack. This is what you hand out when you've finished your presentation and answered all their questions.

FACTS AND FIGURES IN THE TAKE-AWAY PACK

When you hand out your take-away pack, the audience will automatically flick through it and turn to the page that interests them most. Then there's nothing worse than someone in the audience saying, "This doesn't look quite right." Your heart drops like a stone and the blood drains from your face in panic.

The best way to stop this happening is for you to check, double check, and then get someone else to do the same. Preferably someone who can take an objective view of your figures. It's the numbers that

IN THE DRAGONS' DEN, *entrepreneurs are not permitted to use notes to refer to, and many lose track of the numbers or go blank under the pressure of the spotlight. The key figures the Dragons target are turnover and profit over a four to five year period: the previous year or two of trading, the current year and two or three years hence. Like any investor, they are also keen to test the valuation of a company.*

IN YOUR PITCH, *you can have documents and tables of figures to refer to, but it is much better if you can commit the numbers to memory if at all possible, and this is for two reasons. Firstly – if you can list your turnover and profit figures for the current year, the previous two years and projected figures for the next three – it shows that you know your business inside out and have a good grasp of where it's going. Secondly, it allows you to engage more fully with your audience – you can look at them, gauge how they are responding and adjust your presentation as you go.*

KAY RUSSELL *(top, see pp140–1,* **CAROL SAVAGE** *(centre, see p19) and* **MICHAEL COTTON** *(bottom, see pp226–7) all demonstrated an excellent grasp of the important numbers. As Michael Cotton says, "in large part, this was down to an intense period of preparation in the weeks leading up to the pitch."*

" THE FEWER CLEAR FACTS YOU HAVE IN SUPPORT OF AN OPINION, THE STRONGER YOUR EMOTIONAL ATTACHMENT TO THAT OPINION " ANON

" FACTS ARE STUBBORN THINGS, BUT STATISTICS ARE MORE PLIABLE "

MARK TWAIN (1835–1910)

are important. But just because you've produced them in a fancy spreadsheet, it doesn't mean they're correct.

All the facts, figures and back-up information in the pack are probably in your business plan already. But the take-away pack will look different. It will contain copies of your charts and graphs, notes and the raw data from your spreadsheets.

Whichever way you decide to lay it out, you should produce it in a Sans Serif font – that's one that doesn't have the curly bits at the ends of the letters – because that infers factual information without embellishment. Good fonts are Arial or Verdana. The latter is good for blocks of text as it has a slightly wider spacing and is easier on the eye. Arial is good for the numbers in your spreadsheet. If a page consists of text, you should lay it out as two columns to make it easier to read, and make sure that each new topic starts on a new page.

Here's a list of what to include in your take-away pack, which will prove to your audience that you 'know your stuff' and are credible.

- **CONTENTS.** A table of contents, with page numbers, so the audience can quickly find the information they want. This will also help you when you get stuck on a difficult question.

- **THE IDEA.** A one-page description of your idea and the 'magic' technology that makes it different. Also include the problem it solves, a profile of a typical customer and the reasons why people should buy it.

- **THE MARKET.** A clear definition of your market, its size and potential. You'll probably need to express this in terms of quantities and value. This section will probably be two or three pages long.

- **BUSINESS MODEL AND PRICING.** No more than two pages that cover a description of your business model and your proposed pricing structure.

- **THE COMPETITION.** A list of your competitors and their market shares. You will need one page with a pie-chart that shows market shares and a page for each of your major competitors.

- **MARKETING AND SALES PLAN.** A couple of pages that describe how you intend to market and sell your idea or product. Detailed sales projections and marketing costs will be in another section of the document.

- **KEY PEOPLE.** Half-page biographies of each of the senior management team and any other key people in the business. You should also indicate the type and numbers of any additional people you will need to recruit.

- **FINANCIAL PROJECTIONS.** Three or four pages with sales projections and gross margins, marketing and sales costs, and any other operational costs over the next two years. Include a Profit and Loss statement that covers eight

“ CONVINCE ME THERE’S A REASONABLE CHANCE THAT I’LL GET A REASONABLE RETURN ON MY INVESTMENT ”

DUNCAN BANNATYNE, DRAGON

quarters on one sheet, and also a cash flow analysis for the next 12 months.

- **TIME-SCALES.** An activity plan with time-scales that covers sales, marketing, recruitment and procurement over the next 12 to 15 months. You must make sure that you have identified any costs that are associated with these activities in the previous section.

Yes, the take-away pack has a similar structure to your presentation. This has two benefits: it will help you if you need to refer to the pack during the question and answer session; and it will remind the audience of what you talked about during the first 20 minutes.

In summary, your credibility comes from the confidence you have in yourself, your knowledge of the market and your idea, and your track record. You show your confidence by not using a script of notes. You prove your knowledge from the contents of your presentation and take-away pack. And you demonstrate your track record when you explain how you overcame problems in the past and delivered results.

JOSEPHINE BUCHAN

JOSEPHINE'S PITCH *stressed the creative opportunity of the project.*

The Den can be a cruel place for exposing the difference between what you think you've got and what you're actually offering as an investment.

Josephine Buchan went into the Den asking for £250,000 for 25% equity in a production of a musical based on the life and songs of Dusty Springfield. The thrust of her pitch was on the creative side of the project. A song was performed and Josephine was keen to stress that, as the show's producer, she was offering to assemble the best possible creative team to create a successful musical. This was all good, positive stuff – as Deborah Meaden said, "you've won me on the topic". However, the Dragons then fired question after question about the musical's investment potential.

Unaccustomed to investing in the musical industry, the Dragons wanted hard and fast figures and a clear business model. They wanted to know the average number of seats in an average theatre and the average cost of those seats. They wanted to know how much it costs to hire a theatre.

Fair enough questions when you're being asked for £250,000, and you want to forecast the point at which you'll make a profit. But, for Josephine, the answers were too dependent on factors she wouldn't really know until the show had got going: theatre prices are usually negotiable, and the number of tickets they'd be selling was very difficult to predict.

From Josephine's perspective, the success of a show is a far more nebulous affair than the Dragons would accept: if it is well received by audiences and critics, it will play to big theatres, potentially creating large amounts of revenue. If it isn't well received, the whole thing could be pulled within a couple of weeks, with all investment lost. It's not an activity that aims at a middle ground of respectable profitability, and the Dragons pulled out.

THE DRAGONS *may have appreciated the music, but it was clearly a clash of cultures when it came to the business. "Convince me there's a reasonable chance that I'll get a reasonable return on my investment," implored Duncan Bannatyne, while Deborah concluded, "We are speaking a slightly different language."*

JOSEPHINE HAS SINCE ACCRUED *most of the investment from other sources and is in rehearsals of the musical.*

COMMANDMENT 5

USE PROPS

Can you liven up your act?

IT'S ALL VERY WELL TALKING, but as is often said, a picture can be worth a thousand words. The Dragons' Den has seen everything from a diagram glued to a board to a performance with live music and a troupe of dancers. No entrepreneur enters the Den without some kind of prop. Whoever you're pitching a business idea to, if you have a product, bring it. If you're planning a product but haven't made a prototype yet, bring pictures of it. If there's no product, but a service, then mock up a scene with people using the service. There must be *something* you can use as a prop.

Props can be used in three main ways during a presentation:

- **TO FIRE ENTHUSIASM** – product samples in particular help your audience understand what you are excited about.
- **TO ASSIST YOU IN EXPLAINING DETAILS** – market shares and so forth.
- **TO REINFORCE YOUR MESSAGES** – we explain how they can do so in this chapter.

TYPES OF PROP

Ideally you will want to use a variety of props that cover all three communication modes – visual, auditory and kinaesthetic (see Commandment 3). There is so much choice these days, and you don't need to be in a TV studio to come up with some great props. However, you need to be aware of drawbacks with some.

- **PRODUCT SAMPLES.** These are a must – you just have to have them if your pitch is about a product. They work at the emotional level and bring your idea to life. They

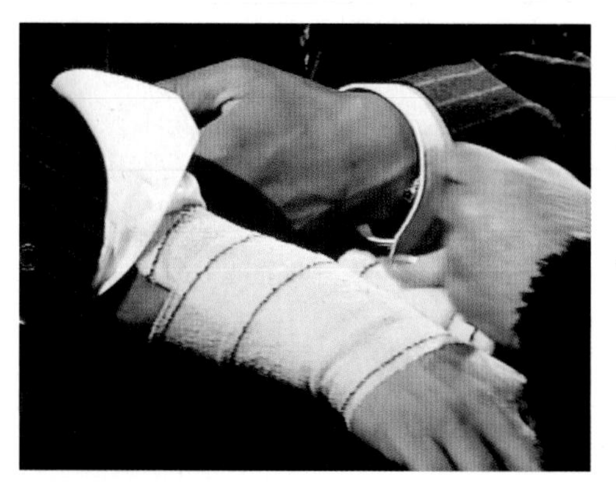

KAY RUSSELL DEMONSTRATED HER PHYSICOOL PRODUCT *(see pp140–1) on James. Unlike with muscle injury sprays that instantly freeze the treated area, Physicool gradually absorbs the heat from around the injury. Through the demonstration James was able to feel the gradual cooling effect of the bandage rather than just be told about it.*

particularly appeal to kinaesthetic people, who form about a third of the typical audience.

- **POWERPOINT.** This widely used tool is probably the first choice for most presenters. But it's all too easy for a PowerPoint presentation to go wrong, and it may not even be appropriate for your pitch. The biggest problem is usually the challenge of the technology itself, especially if you're planning to take your PowerPoint presentation on a memory stick or your laptop to use with someone else's projection equipment. See pp107–8.

- **VIDEO.** A short film showing the product or service in action, or customers talking about it, can be very effective. You only have to spend some time on YouTube to see what you can do with a decent digital camera, a tripod, some good lighting and a cheap piece of video editing software. Again, though, there will be a technological challenge simply in making your audio-visual equipment work in the presentation setting.

- **OVERHEADS.** Yes, an overhead projector is old-fashioned technology but it is very flexible. You can have professional-looking slides onto which you can scribble with a marker pen when you want to highlight a point and show off your enthusiasm. You can also easily change the order of your material on the fly and have slides in your bag that you've prepared to use in the Q&A session at the end.

- **WHITEBOARD OR FLIP CHART.** Some people think these low-tech tools are a bit amateurish. But you have a certain power when you spontaneously write things on a board or flip chart. Your passion and enthusiasm will come across and what they won't know is that you planned what you're writing days earlier.

- **CHARTS OR BOARDS.** By this we mean A2 pieces of thick white card with graphics, pictures or charts stuck on to them with glue. You can place them on an easel or flip chart stand to show them to your audience, or you can hold them against your chest. The nice thing is you can have two or three up at one time and use them almost like a pack of cards. Or you can lean them up against the wall on tables around the room. Advertising agencies and design consultancies are very fond of boards and use them to sell their ideas and concepts with great success.

- **OTHER PROPS.** Be as creative as you can with anything else that the audience can see and touch. You can use all manner of props as analogies and ways to punch your message home. For example, Jamie Oliver, the television celebrity chef, once emptied a sack of sugar cubes onto the floor to show how much sugar children consume in a year. It made his message about children's unhealthy eating habits very vivid and was much more powerful and memorable than just having a number or diagram on a board or projector.

MICHAEL NORTH, THE SELF-STYLED OLIVE MAN *(see pp160–1) got the Dragons to indulge in a tasting session, to compare a premium supermarket olive oil with a fresh bottle that he had selected from a recent harvest. This gave the Dragons a chance to experience what he was desperately trying to convey: that "fresh seasonal olive oil" has at least as great a complexity of flavours as wine and that there is a real difference between olive oils readily available in supermarkets today and the kind of fresh oils that he would provide in his proposed olive oil club. For, unlike wine, which can mature over time, olive oil is always better the fresher it is consumed.*

PETER JONES *was particularly taken with the tasting, expressing delight when he felt the pepper kick at the back of his palate that Michael had described. "You're a little dehydrated," Michael explained, "because you experienced it late." Peter was amazed to discover this and dutifully took a sip of water to top up his aqua levels.*

OVERALL *the pitch didn't convince the Dragons that there was enough of an investment opportunity to take a stake in the business, but by sampling good oil and contrasting it with supermarket offerings, they could at least appreciate that there was a reason for the business and that it could tap in to a niche market for discerning foodies.*

CASE STUDY **FROM SERIES 7 EPISODE 2**

BASSTONESLAP

This was a dynamic pitch, in which Richard Enion and Michael Davis decided to give the Dragons a feel of their business: a drumming workshop for corporate team building, performances and 'experiential marketing' (a kind of branded performance). They launched into a display, with around a dozen drummers creating a big, powerful sound, then encouraged the Dragons to get up and have a go on the skins themselves.

It was a valuable part of the pitch but the Dragons' also needed a sound business reason for investing in BassToneSlap. The turning

THE GROUP HAVE BEEN CONCENTRATING *more on drumming performances than corporate team building events since their appearance in the Den.*

point of the pitch came when the duo mentioned that similar franchises had been sold for as much as £100,000.

Peter and Theo made a joint offer which reflected the potential they saw in the duo, but also the work needed to make BassToneSlap a marketable franchise. Because of this, the Dragons' offer was for a high equity stake (40%) – four times the figure that Richard and Michael had originally offered.

AFTER A ROUSING PERFORMANCE, *BassToneSlap encouraged the Dragons to pick up the sticks and have a go for themselves. For four of the Dragons, and for Deborah, Theo and Peter in particular, it gave an immediate and visceral sense of how drumming could work for corporate clients as a fun team building exercise.*

OF COURSE, CAJOLING POTENTIAL INVESTORS *to join in with a group activity can be a risky strategy, and it certainly alienated Duncan Bannatyne, but encouraging participation is the nature of the BassToneSlap business, and they did manage to lure two Dragons into investing. Michael and Richard gave it some consideration, as it was for far more equity than they had offered, but in the end agreed to the deal.*

ANTHONY COATES-SMITH AND ALISTAIR TURNER *brought a map mounted on a board as one of their props during their pitch for Igloo in Series 4 (see p209). It reinforced the point that, with two extra operating hubs, they could service customers throughout England and Wales.*

THE MAGIC WHITEBOARD *in Series 6 was itself the product sample as well as visual prop (see also p196). The Dragons could see how easy it was to put up and use. Peter, baffled by the simplicity of the Magic Whiteboard, used it to declare himself "out", while Deborah wrote "Thankyou Duncan" to another Dragon.*

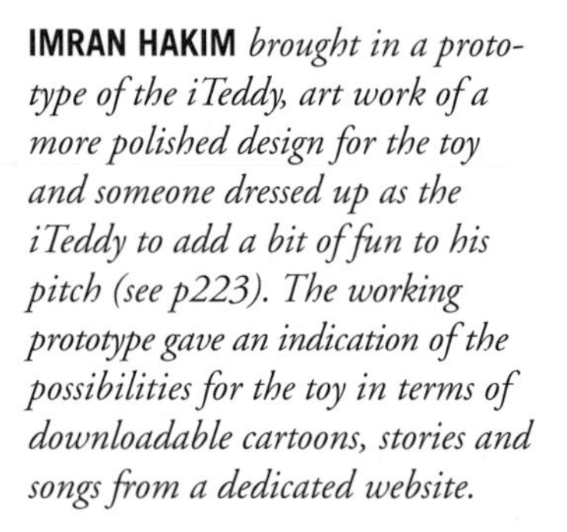

IMRAN HAKIM *brought in a prototype of the iTeddy, art work of a more polished design for the toy and someone dressed up as the iTeddy to add a bit of fun to his pitch (see p223). The working prototype gave an indication of the possibilities for the toy in terms of downloadable cartoons, stories and songs from a dedicated website.*

THE TROUBLE WITH POWERPOINT

For those entrepreneurial readers who *don't* come from a corporate background, where PowerPoint is ubiquitous, we should explain first that PowerPoint is a piece of software made by Microsoft that operates as a slide show using a computer and digital projector. Presenters can potentially show photographs, diagrams, text, audio clips and video clips with the equipment. Templates are provided by PowerPoint to help lay out multimedia slides, which can be customized with a company logo.

PowerPoint is easy to learn, which is both its strength and its weakness. Because so many corporate presentations use PowerPoint templates and accoutrements, they have little creative edge. Too many people write their presentation straight into PowerPoint without much thought. The result is usually disjointed and feels unprofessional to the audience.

No film or TV director will point a camera until they are very clear about each scene and why they need it. They will have storyboarded every single shot and you must do the same if you want to use PowerPoint. Just because you can quickly build flying text and fanfares, doesn't mean you should. Similarly there's no need to put a logo on the corner of each slide. It doesn't do anything for the audience – it just says you're like everyone else. If you dress up your slides with all the PowerPoint bells and whistles, you will dilute your message. Don't forget they've seen it all before, and you don't want to come across as mutton dressed up as lamb.

Then there are issues with the technology. You don't want to eat into your allocated time by fiddling with kit, and panicking about why it won't work. More importantly, you'll lose the power and end up on the back foot if your audience is impatiently waiting for you to start. So make especially sure that you have a compelling reason to use PowerPoint when the pitch is not on your own premises.

USE TELEVISION AS YOUR LEAD

In the time of Charles Dickens and Jane Austen people were happy to sit through a three-hour speech or sermon. They listened and understood without the need for any visual aids and other props. Now it's all different, and that's mainly because of television.

Television has had a massive impact on our lives and no more so than in the way we communicate. We're conditioned to receiving information in small 'soundbites'. Our brains now look forward to the ad break so it can take a bit of a rest. We get bored very quickly if the image remains the same.

- **ACCEPT THAT THE BAR HAS BEEN RAISED.** These days we expect a performance from speakers and entertainers because our standards and expectations are much higher – because of television. We've become used to watching professionals using slick graphics and props. They have set the bar up high, and because of that your pitch will fail if your performance seems indifferent and your props amateurish. An 'okay' presentation is not enough; you have to give a sparkling performance to impress.

- **UNDERSTAND CHUNKING.** Think about a television documentary or a news programme. The topics and stories are the big picture – overviews. It's called

RAYMOND SMITH'S PITCH FOR THE MAGIC PIZZA *was extremely nervy and the type of product initially left the Dragons bemused to the point of not knowing whether it was a serious pitch or not. The Magic Pizza is a perforated metal disc that sits under a pizza as it cooks, raising up the central portion to eliminate what Raymond referred to as a recognized problem in the frozen pizza industry – that of the "soggy middle". The Dragons were sceptical that this was a problem crying out for a design solution. The best way to dispel those doubts would have been to demonstrate the clear superiority of a frozen pizza cooked with a Magic Pizza over one cooked without the device. Cue Raymond's cook and taste demonstration.*

UNFORTUNATELY, *the pizzas' cooking times hadn't been handled correctly, and both were overcooked – a fact that Raymond pointed out only after Duncan had given his assessment that he couldn't tell the difference. Despite the demonstration seriously undermining the pitch and despite Raymond's less than convincing presentation, the Magic Pizza secured investment from Peter and Theo. The reason: that Raymond had patented his invention, so, if it did take off, he would have a monopoly in the market.*

'chunking'. The chunks are a couple of minutes long with a short and clear explanation. Often they mention a website address for those people who want more details. It's rare to see a person who just talks straight to the camera for longer than about a minute. 'Chunking' happens in other media too. Look at how newspapers, especially the tabloids, break up information. Look at how this very paragraph, labelled 'Understand Chunking' is separated from those around it. However, it is on television documentaries and news that 'chunking' has been turned into an art form with the use of visual aids.

" I VISUALIZE THINGS IN MY MIND BEFORE I HAVE TO DO THEM. IT IS LIKE HAVING A MENTAL WORKSHOP. "

JACK YOUNGBLOOD, AUTHOR

- **SEE HOW THE VISUAL REINFORCES THE MESSAGE.** Next time you watch the news or a documentary on television, look at what happens when there's a chart or graphic on screen – the narrator always explains what it's about. In this way, the visual prop goes hand-in-hand with the spoken words in the 'chunk'. What you're looking at is reinforced by the 'message', and vice-versa. You can take inspiration from some of the ideas and techniques of professional television presenters for your own presentation.

USING VISUALS SUCH AS ILLUSTRATIONS AND TEXT

A very common presentation technique is to show a series of visuals that reinforce the subjects being talked about. This can be a good way of 'chunking'. The visuals can be shown on a flip chart, whiteboard, overhead projector or PowerPoint. Charts, illustrations and even written text can be used as visuals. Indeed, you can think of your visuals as like the headlines and subheads in a newspaper or magazine article; the words you speak as like the outline of the article; and your take-away pack as the details.

We keep emphasizing in this book that the presentation part of your pitch should ideally be about 20 minutes. If you are indeed planning to present for this duration of time, we'd suggest that you limit the number of visuals to 10 – any more than that will probably be too many for your audience to take in properly.

Here are some tips about using visuals:

- **WORK OUT YOUR VISUALS ON STICKIES.** Novice presenters usually try to cram far too much onto each visual. To avoid this, take 10 stickies, one for each visual, and stick them on the wall. Then, with a pencil and your original storyboard in front of you, write the contents of each visual on the stickies. If the sticky isn't big enough, then you're trying to fit on too much.

USE STICKIES TO PLAN YOUR VISUALS

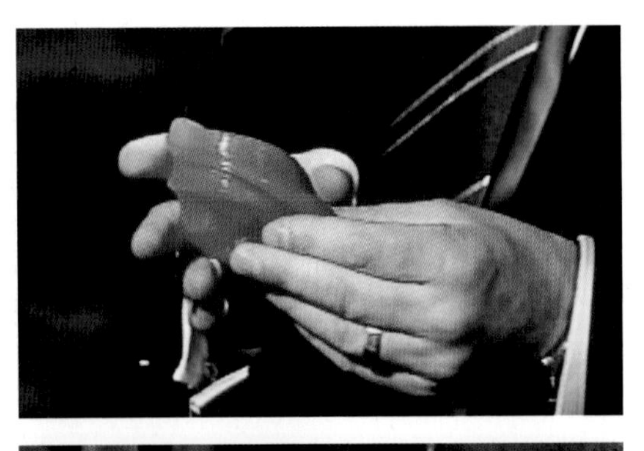

IN SERIES 7, JASON ROBERTS PITCHED FOR TECH 21, *a company that specialized in producing mobile and laptop protective cases. There in the Den he demonstrated the unique properties of a fabric called d3o, which is incorporated into Tech 21's products. Firstly Jason used a lump of orange d3o to demonstrate its pliable qualities, showing that it could be moulded into any number of forms. Then he demonstrated how its molecules lock together on impact to form a strong, protective substance. To show this in action, he hit the lump of d3o with a hammer and threw a mobile phone onto the table and floor to show how its case prevented any damage. The Dragons had already admired the look of the cases; now they could see for themselves how well the technology in the materials performed.*

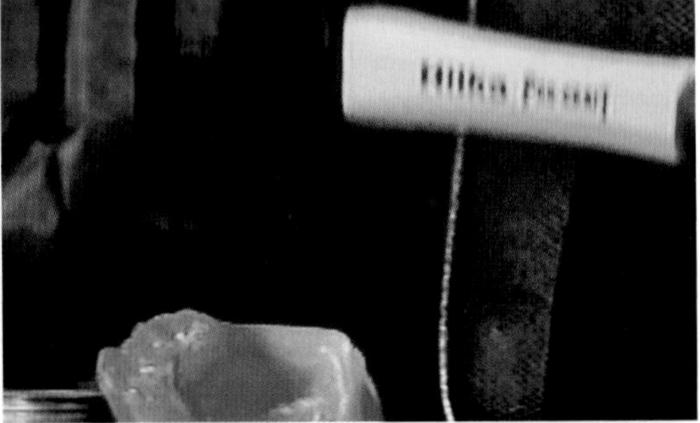

- **REMEMBER YOUR VISUALS ARE NOT YOUR SCRIPT.** Any visuals with text should be acting as the 'headline', not just a repeat of what you're saying.

- **LIMIT THE NUMBER OF LISTS.** Bullet points are a good way to highlight the main points, but don't abuse them. A long list of things is just a lazy way of putting information across. It does not demonstrate your emotion and your passion.

- **USE SIMPLE AND CLEAR CHARTS OR GRAPHS.** Don't clutter them with too much information. You will be explaining to the audience what the chart shows in order to empathize with the Auditories in the audience. Practise using a pointer if you need to.

- **KEEP POWERPOINT VISUALS SIMPLE.** If you're going to be using PowerPoint, make sure your slides have a plain background with lots of 'white space' and no clutter. Always pick a Sans Serif font that has no curly bits and try and find one that is widely spaced so the individual characters are easy to read (see p92). Never use text that's all capitals – it's like shouting and it's hard to understand. Use a 28- or 30-point font so you're forced to keep the words to the absolute minimum. Some people say that you should have no more than five points per slide, and five words per point. The general rule is: the fewer, the better.

WHEN TO SHOW AND WHEN TO TELL

Some parts of your pitch will need visuals and some won't. Bear these points in mind when planning your visuals.

- **DATA, FACTS AND QUOTES**

  SHOW Data, figures, facts and quotes from famous people are best displayed on visuals.

  TELL If you're showing a quote visually, then in this instance you can also read it out loud to push the message home.

- **GRAPHS AND CHARTS**

  SHOW You can use graphs or charts that cover market shares, growth projections and sales figures. But only put a summary on the visual because the details and actual numbers will be in the take-away pack.

  TELL However, when a chart or graph appears on the screen you will need to explain what it's about and what it means. While you do that you should change the tone of your voice so it is more authoritarian or factual rather than your normal voice. You want to use a 'matter of fact' voice. This will reinforce the message that it's true and appeal to the logical part of their brain.

- **ANECDOTES**

  TELL Stories, analogies and anecdotes are best just spoken. If you're using PowerPoint you can prompt the audience to listen by blanking out the screen. The best way to do this is to press the 'B' key; you can press any other key to bring it back. Or you can have a filler slide such as a photograph of your product or your premises. If you're using a flip chart, cover it up. With an overhead, turn it off. You should also draw the audience into your story by changing the tone of your voice. Slow down and put on your 'let me tell you a story' voice. Make it warmer and softer and move nearer the audience – your voice has become the 'prop' at this point.

ALLOW FOR THE SHIFTS IN POWER

Think about how magicians or children's entertainers work. They come on stage with their magical box that contains all their tricks, and they take them out one at a time. They have the power because the audience has to wait for them each time. However, when they bring something out of the bag, the audience's attention goes to the object, and the entertainer loses a bit of power.

You will be handing over some power to your audience when you take out your product samples. Allow them to play with them for a bit while you observe them in silence. You'll recognize the kinaesthetic people because their eyes will light up as they touch and feel them. Then take control again as you continue talking.

Similarly, when you unveil a new visual, you need to stop talking for a couple of seconds, to create a pause as the power shifts. This allows your audience to absorb and assimilate the information that you've just unveiled on the visual. Often you'll see them shift their gaze back to you when they've taken it all in. This is a signal for you to explain what it's all about and what it means.

Because the power shifts when you show a visual, you need to choose visuals with great care. Make sure they all support your argument and reinforce your message. The last thing you want is for a visual to raise other points or send the audience off at a tangent or different direction. Make sure that although the power temporarily shifts, you don't lose control.

Under no circumstances must you hand out copies of your take-away pack at the start of your presentation. If you do, the audience will jump ahead – the financial people will immediately turn to the Profit and Loss statement and cash flow analysis, and everyone else will start flicking through the pack, stopping at anything that catches their eye. If that happens, you've handed over far too much power to the audience and effectively lost control.

FINAL THOUGHTS

The audience will almost certainly go away remembering your product samples most of all, followed by any other physical props that you bring in, and finally your visuals. They might be able to recall your stories and anecdotes, but not much else of what you've actually said. Therefore, it is very important that you allow plenty of time to devise and practise with your props so you are totally comfortable with them. This is especially the case with anything that requires turning on and off, and you should work out a backup plan of what to do if a technology prop such as PowerPoint doesn't work on the day.

PAPER BLINDS *from the Blinds In A Box entrepreneurs Simeone Salik, Janice Dalton and Dominic Lawrence were demonstrated in Series 6, giving the Dragons a chance to see for themselves how quickly and easily they can be put up (see also p59).*

DRAGON THEO PAPHITIS *broke the Rapstrap cable tie in Series 6 (see p39), but Duncan Bannatyne and James Caan invested in the company, Duncan pointing out that you can pull buttons off a shirt too, but it doesn't mean that buttons don't work.*

VERNON KERSWELL *brought in a sample of one of his Extreme Fliers in Series 7 (see p127). Vernon flew the remote control model insect in the Den and then let a happy Theo have a go too.*

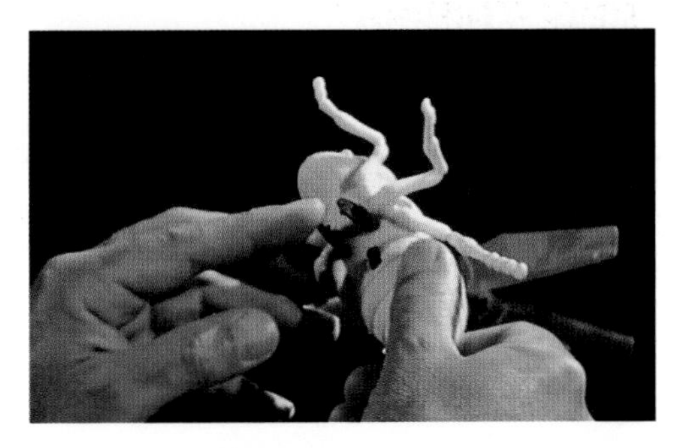

A DEVICE *to prevent cars from misfuelling was a product sample shown by Michael Cotton in Series 6 (see pp226–7). Although they didn't see it working, the Dragons got to grips with the principle of the product and the way it would work when fitted.*

CASE STUDY **FROM SERIES 7 EPISODE 6**

GRILLSTREAM

As you would expect when facing the fearsome Dragons, Peter Neath and Ian Worton were slightly ill at ease when they first went into the Den to pitch for investment in their Grillstream invention. However, once they were able to demonstrate the process of this new type of grill – in which fat from cooking meat that would otherwise drip into the grill pan, or directly onto the coals of a barbecue if cooking outdoors, is instead siphoned off along narrow tubes to a collection tray – they were able to relax a little, confident in the knowledge that both the product and the props used to demonstrate its method worked perfectly. And when Deborah wanted to test the grill further, unsure whether the quality of the product was sufficiently detailed, it proved itself up to the task.

SOMEWHAT NERVOUSLY, *Peter Neath and Ian Worton begin their pitch in the Den.*

The presentation had demonstrated the credibility of the product, and the Dragons, Peter and Theo in particular, seemed impressed. Ultimately, though, Peter Neath and Ian Worton didn't get the £120,000 investment they were looking for. Theo came closest to investing, but concluded that it was an invention that needed licensing to oven and barbecue manufacturers rather than attempting to produce and market it as a separate product to replace existing grill pans.

Prior to visiting the Den, the Midlands-based duo had looked into the possibility of licensing the Grillstream, but without knowledge of this kind of business they were looking for a Dragon to steer them through the process. Having not got one on board, they persevered themselves and have since struck a deal with a manufacturer of barbecues. Not content with licensing, though, they have also continued to manufacture, as a separate product, the Grillstream that they demonstrated in the Den.

IN THE SIMPLE DEMONSTRATION *Peter dripped a coloured liquid over a toy sausage on a standard grill and on the Grillstream. The contrast was clear: on the Grillstream no coloured liquid dripped through. Deborah wanted to test if it wasn't in perfect alignment and, again, it worked fine. Theo liked the product but could only conclude that its future lay in a licensing deal with an oven or barbecue manufacturer.*

COMMANDMENT 6

LEARN TO LOVE QUESTIONS

Are you prepared for them?

IF YOU'VE WATCHED MANY EPISODES of Dragons' Den, you'll know that questions are fired at participants after they've had the opportunity to give their presentation. Some questions come up quite predictably, probing financial forecasts for example. Canny entrepreneurs memorize key figures to throw back at the Dragons. Other questions catch participants unawares – they don't know the answer offhand, or it uncovers something that throws a different light on the business proposal. You need to think hard about what questions are likely to be asked and how you'll respond to them. You won't be able to anticipate every question, but this chapter shows you how to respond in any situation, even when you don't know the answers.

A major element for a successful pitch is how you connect with the audience. Some of this is about your body language when you stand there and speak, which we will cover in Commandment 8. Some of it is how you respond to questions from the audience.

Many presenters are wary, if not terrified, of questions – and you'll probably feel the same to begin with. But actually questions are a good sign as they show that the audience is interested. When the audience takes an active part in the proceedings you know your pitch is going well. It's like a television programme where they laugh and clap because they are enjoying themselves. So get it in your head that questions aren't interruptions, they're actually audience participation. They are like a 'thumbs up' sign from the audience.

QUESTIONS ARE AN OPPORTUNITY

The question and answer session is your chance as the presenter to show off your knowledge and expertise. You can add information to enhance your message and show that you're confident enough to respond to their queries. Only a person who knows their subject is willing to take questions, and you will gain a lot of credibility if you can respond well to questions.

Having said that, questions empower the audience – the power shifts to the person asking the question before it returns to you as you answer it. You can understand the power shift if you understand the underlying reasons why people ask questions during a pitch.

1 **SEEKING CLARIFICATION AND MORE DETAIL.** This is ostensibly what the question is about. They want you to clarify something you said or they want more information

MICHAEL PRITCHARD'S PITCH *(left) for the Anyway Spray encountered a surprising amount of turbulence in the Den, but he used the questioning as a way to turn things around and win investment. Though the Anyway Spray worked better than a conventional dip tube in sprays and aerosols (see also p84), the Dragons weren't convinced that manufacturers would readily adopt a new tube that would cost them an extra penny on each can or bottle (the cost of licensing the Anyway tube from Michael) and, as Duncan pointed out, the product was worth nothing unless the manufacturers were prepared to buy or license the Anyway tube.*

THREE DRAGONS HAD ALREADY RULED THEMSELVES OUT, WHEN PETER *(left) began reiterating his concerns about the business's viability. This time, though, Michael was able to counter with a financial benefit for the manufacturers of aerosols – that, because his spray worked with compressed air rather than VOCs such as butane, this would result in a cost benefit to the manufacturers. Michael then leapt on a point that Peter began to make regarding disposal. "That's a very good question. There's a big cost in disposal with these aerosols. Councils will only take them if they are empty, so they have to go through a very rigid disposal programme because they've got flammable gases … with the Anyway tube they could recycle them without going through the costly process of removing the propane and butane." It was a convincing argument that won Peter over; Theo too, and the two Dragons made a joint offer of investment.*

or detail about a particular item or topic. In other words they are using the power of questioning to go further down the pyramid (see pp89–90).

2. **GAUGING YOU AS A PERSON.** The people you are pitching to want to know more about your character and personality to decide if they can work with you. They are using their power to make you respond in ways that should reveal this to them.

3. **DISPUTING WHAT YOU'VE SAID.** They might feel confused about a point, or dispute some of your facts and will use the power of questioning to make this known to you and the rest of the room. Unfortunately some people can get tenacious and will relentlessly pursue a point.

4. **SELF-PROMOTION.** Yes, questioners may well want to make an impression in front of their peers. They may be more interested in furthering their own status through questioning rather than the actual answer to a question.

YOU CAN SET THE RULES AT THE START

You might decide that the best time for questions is at the end of your presentation, because that will allow you to bring everything together, and questions from your audience won't interrupt your flow. If you want to set a definite Q&A session at the end, state this at the start. Bear in mind, though, that when you put off a Q&A session to the end, you don't have the opportunity to get direct feedback on what the audience is thinking as you're going along. Also, you may get a few questions anyway. If someone interrupts you with a burning question, you must deal with it there and then. Do not say "I'll answer that at the end" as it sounds like you're just fobbing them off. If, however, you cover that point in the next few slides, say so. But make sure that you do actually respond to their specific question when you get to the appropriate slide.

" IT IS BETTER TO KNOW SOME OF THE QUESTIONS THAN ALL OF THE ANSWERS "

JAMES THURBER, AMERICAN AUTHOR, CARTOONIST & SATIRIST

If you want, you can allow questions at any time. Indeed, if you've rehearsed your presentation and have learnt the flow, you should be able to take questions on the hoof. Let your audience know at the beginning if you're happy to take questions at any point. Not only will you be getting instant feedback but you will also be demonstrating to the audience that you're confident. There is a drawback of taking any questions during your presentation, though, in that you will lose a bit of control for a while each time.

There is another way. At the very start of your presentation you could explain what you're going to talk about and then you say something like, "I suggest that we have a question and answer session at the end. However, please interrupt if you have any burning issues and I'll try and answer them as we go along." Then a couple of times

THE DRAGONS CLEARLY ENJOYED VERNON KERSWELL'S PITCH *(see opposite), none more so than Theo Paphitis, a self-confessed 'big kid'. From the off, Theo was itching to get his hands on the remote control and take the Extreme Fliers Terror Wasp out for a spin.*

WHAT THE DRAGONS LIKED ABOUT VERNON *was not just that he had put so much effort into his project – going to work in a Chinese factory and picking up enough Mandarin to get by en route – but that he enjoyed the whole process so thoroughly. Determination is a good thing in business, but for an entrepreneur unbridled enthusiasm is unsurpassable.*

in your presentation, before you move on to a new topic, you can ask if they have any questions at that point. Don't ask this all the time or it will look like you need lots of reassurance. As with any communication technique it's about striking the right balance.

NOTHING BEATS PREPARATION

No politician would dream of meeting the press without preparing. You need to do the same. Public relations companies and publicists always prepare their clients with a list of questions to expect along with the answers to them. The night before the press interview the

CASE STUDY **FROM SERIES 7 EPISODE 8**

VERNON KERSWELL

Despite being one of the youngest entrepreneurs to enter the Den, Vernon had the confidence to speak with tremendous enthusiasm about the remote-controlled flying toys he'd been developing.

VERNON *subsequently obtained investment and went into production with the Terror Wasp in time for Christmas 2009.*

Questions about pricing he answered clearly and concisely, and when asked about the background to his business venture he became expansive in his reply. Switching to story-teller mode, he described how he'd taken a year out of his university studies to go to China, learn Mandarin and work in a factory developing prototype toys – something he clearly relished. He described how he and his Chinese colleagues would work late into the night, then get up early the next day to start all over again. In so doing, he painted a picture of someone dedicated, energetic, inventive and cooperative – all adding to his credibility and investability.

Though Vernon didn't get the investment he wanted on this occasion, his presentation proved him to be an eminently investable individual, who mixed a bright, ingenious mind with sound business sense.

interviewee will spend time going through these, so they understand the tone and content of the answers to give. Of course you should never give your list of questions and answers to the audience. It's for your own and your team's use only.

One of the reasons you bounced your storyboard off your friend is to get an idea of the questions that you might be asked. You should also be able to work out other likely questions if you've taken the time to understand the audience and the background of each person there. Think about their particular experience and areas of expertise. This will give you some idea of the things that they will be concerned about. Write down the questions and answers and rehearse them so you get them in your head.

If the answer is in your take-away pack, then try and remember what page it's on so you can point them to it or get the information yourself and tell them. That will make you look very knowledgeable and confident. If you can't think where it is, look it up in the table of contents at the front of the pack.

BASIC RULES FOR ANSWERING QUESTIONS

There are a few simple techniques that you should bear in mind when you get to the question and answer part of your pitch.

- **CULTIVATE CALMNESS.** At the start of the Q&A session get yourself in a positive mental state by taking slow breaths. The key word is slow, rather than deep – in fact, don't breathe deeply into your chest as you will stimulate the fight and flight reflex which produces adrenaline. You need to be calm, not wound up like a spring.

- **DON'T ANSWER TOO QUICKLY.** Suppress your emotions and don't automatically respond to a question without pausing and thinking about it first. Try and see the question from the questioner's point of view and feed their self-interest with an answer in a positive light.

- **LEARN TO RECOGNIZE WHAT'S BEHIND THEIR QUESTIONS.** It could be that they want you to clarify a particular point. Or they want more details about a particular aspect of your pitch. In the worst case, they could be questioning the validity of your argument or data.

- **BE COMFORTABLE WITH SILENCE.** Do not give them any more information than they've particularly asked for. You do not want to drift beyond the point or raise other questions in their mind. If you can, try and link back to other things you said previously. But never say, "I covered that before" (even if you did) as that implies that they weren't really listening.

- **NEVER EVER USE THE WORD "SORRY".** Finally, do not apologize for something you've done or haven't said.

CONTROL YOUR BODY WHEN LISTENING TO QUESTIONS

We look at your personal appearance and general body language in Commandment 8. What you need to know here is that the Q&A session can be the most dangerous part in terms of your personal body language. The biggest challenge is when you're actually listening to a question – it's all too easy to give away feelings of insecurity at that point. You will have to suppress your emotions, put a neutral mask on your face and control your movements.

Practise the bodily stance and movements described below in front of a mirror until they feel natural. Also rope in your friend to fire questions at you while you practise both answering them and maintaining your composure.

- **HOW TO ADOPT A RELAXED STANCE.** Roll your shoulders back so your arms are slightly raised and your chest is out. Keep one leg straight and bend the other one slightly at the knee. To do this you will need to turn your foot out so your hip doesn't tilt and all your weight is on your straight leg. You are sitting on one hip and it makes you look relaxed and confident. Try always to stand like this when you're listening. Do not start to lean forward or backwards, or let either of your shoulders sag downwards to one side.

PATTI BAILEY OF MOTORMOUSE *(see pp186–7) made a deliberate movement to turn and face each questioner in the Den. She held a steady gaze and spoke clearly and directly in what was an extremely confident pitch.*

- **HOW TO SHOW THAT YOU'RE LISTENING.** Turn to face the person asking the question and concentrate on what they're saying. Stand still like a cat waiting for the mouse to come out, as this will give them the impression of your undivided attention. Try and nod occasionally to show that you're listening. Move slightly towards them or incline your head slightly. This sends a signal that they're the most important person in the room. You should try and create the impression that you're in conversation with them. Remember that when they ask the question, they have the power and you can acknowledge that by moving towards them.

- **WHAT TO DO WITH YOUR ARMS.** The best thing to do is slightly raise the arm that's next to your straight leg and place your other hand on your thigh just above your bent leg. Or gently rest it against your hip. What you're trying to avoid is standing there with your arms down by your side looking rigid, vulnerable or anxious with clenched fists. Don't have your hands behind your back or stand with your hands akimbo on your hips as this is a sign of aggression. And avoid standing with your arms folded as this will make you look defensive.

- **WHAT TO DO WITH YOUR HANDS.** If you put your hands together you'll probably instinctively play with your fingers or a piece of jewellery, whereas if you're standing in the 'relaxed stance' with one hand placed on the top

THE RICHMOND BROTHERS OF SERVICING STOP *(see also p66) stood in perfect unison during their pitch. There was no fidgeting or other distracting movements, which implied a confidence, although the hands clasped in front of them displayed a slightly closed posture – it brought to mind football players forming a defensive wall before a free kick.*

of your leg, you won't be able to fiddle with anything. Alternatively, try placing the back of one hand in the palm of the other in front of you. But raise them up so they're level with your stomach and not over your genital area as that would be a sign that you feel vulnerable. Also try to avoid touching your face with your fingers whilst you're listening to a question or answering. Many people believe strongly that touching behind the ears, or the side of the nose, or the mouth and throat is a sign of deception, and that you're trying to hide something. (Think of the proverbial Three Wise Monkeys – see no evil, hear no evil and speak no evil.) On the other hand, it's probably quite natural for someone to touch their face with their fingers in the pause between question and answer, and some people would recognize this as a positive sign. If in doubt, practise suppressing any urges to touch your face.

- **WHAT TO DO WITH YOUR EYES.** A good steady gaze is important. Keep your head still and level. Look at the person asking the question, but do not stare. Try and look at their whole face and defocus your eyes. You mustn't

PAUL TINTON OF CONSTRUCTION WASTE RECYCLING FIRM PROWASTE *(see p61) kept a notably calm composure and a steady gaze as he answered the Dragons' questions, suggesting an openness and honesty in his responses. This is a very important factor in building a feeling of trust between the entrepreneur and potential investors.*

let your eyes wander around the room when listening to their question, or you will seem shifty, untrustworthy and insincere. Definitely do not look at the floor, as that's regarded everywhere as a classic sign of avoidance and deception. Look at the questioner when you start to answer and then look at everyone else in the room. Finish your answer as you look back at the person who asked the original question.

- **WHAT TO DO WITH YOUR FACIAL EXPRESSIONS.** Whilst listening to a question, generally mask your facial expressions. Don't frown or you'll look worried. Raised eyebrows will make you look curious. Or if you raise just one eyebrow, it'll look like you're suspicious of their intentions. It's okay to smile and laugh during your pitch if you get into a conversation that warrants it, but remember to go back to the neutral mask when you're listening.

HANDLE QUESTIONS IN SEVEN STEPS

When a potential investor asks you a question, there may be several underlying reasons and elements at play, as mentioned on pages 122–4. Then your reaction to the question and how you deal with it are just as important as what you actually say – some people believe they are even more important than what you say.

Follow these seven simple steps, whatever the question is.

1 Turn towards the person asking the question and look at them. Concentrate on them and nod occasionally to show them that you're listening.

2 Demonstrate that you take their question seriously by suppressing your own emotions. Follow the advice about controlling your stance, facial expressions, hands and arms on pages 129–133.

3 Listen intently and don't interrupt. Imagine they're giving you a piece of vital information such as the phone number of someone that you're desperate to contact. Notice the tone of their voice. Is it genuine, insecure or hostile? Try and work out what the point of their question is and what they really want to know.

4 Clarify the question if it sounds obtuse or complex. Sometimes people jumble up two or three points in a single question. If they do, say something like, "Let me just check. You're asking if...?"

"SOMETIMES THE QUESTIONS ARE COMPLICATED BUT THE ANSWERS ARE SIMPLE"

DR SEUSS, AMERICAN AUTHOR & ILLUSTRATOR

5 Pause for a second then answer the question clearly and distinctly in a serious sounding voice. Show empathy and respect by saying something like, "I know it can be a bit confusing" or "that's a good point, let me..." Do not attack the person who asked the question or put them in their place. Audiences have much more in common with each other than they do with you. If you alienate one, they will all gang up against you.

6 Address the rest of the room when you answer the question.

7 When you've finished, stop and smile at the person who asked the question. Slightly tilt your head as though you're asking them if it's okay. They may say "Thank you." If they don't you must check that they are happy with the answer you've given. You should say something like, "Does that answer your question?" If they don't look sure, ask them what else concerns them. But do not get into a long debate with just one member of the audience because it will just annoy everyone else.

GIVE AN HONEST ANSWER

When you answer any question you must tell the truth, but not necessarily the whole truth. You have the power when you answer the question and you don't have to tell them everything. Give them an answer to exactly what they asked and nothing more. You don't want to set them off at a tangent or raise more questions in their mind.

If someone asks what you consider to be a stupid question, do not dismiss them. It's too easy to make a flippant reply and then look around the room with, "Are there any other questions?" This will alienate them and you want friends, not enemies.

WHEN YOU'RE NOT SURE OF THE ANSWER

Even with all the best preparation in the world and a strong presentation, you might be asked a question you haven't prepared for, where you 'go blank' and are not sure how to respond.

If this happens, trust your instincts. Often what we do is think of an answer and rehearse it in our head while we stand there looking worried. We don't feel happy with the first answer so we try and think of another as we feel the butterflies rising in our stomach. But in fact our brain will work out the right words to say as we start to talk. We don't need to rehearse it in our head before we open our mouth. Trust yourself that if you start to answer a question, your

MICHAEL NORTH *(see pp160–1) struggled to answer questions about his projected figures for turnover and profit.*

" WHICH PLANET ARE YOU CURRENTLY ORBITING? IS IT ONE I'M FAMILIAR WITH? "

JAMES CAAN, DRAGON

instinct will take over and you will probably answer it satisfactorily. Many professional speakers train their brain into thinking quickly when under pressure. We'll look at what you can do to improve your brain under stress or pressure in Commandment 9.

When you really don't know the answer to a question about some piece of information or a fact, then it's okay – and possibly the best policy – to admit you don't know. (But, as mentioned earlier in this Commandment, don't use the word "Sorry".) Say something like, "I don't have that information with me at the moment," or, "I can't answer that question at the moment." Then say, "But I will find out the answer and come back to you tomorrow. Is that all right?" This is a reasonable tactic, but you won't be able to use it more than a couple of times as it will soon start to dent your credibility and show them that you're not really prepared on your facts and figures.

Another thing you can do when you don't know the answer is to use the Power of Three that you met in Commandment 4. Reiterate your original point, explain why and finish with an example. (So the three are 'Point, Reason, Example'.) You could say something like, "That's a very interesting point. I think that... because... for example when I looked into... ."

DEALING WITH DIFFICULT QUESTIONS

You should prepare for the possibility of a serious challenge. (Watch Dragons' Den for examples!) If it happens you must remain calm and suppress your emotions. Take a shallow breath, raise yourself up slightly and clench your feet so you're on your toes. Listen carefully with that neutral face we described earlier.

One scenario might be that an expert in the audience attacks your authority. They will tell you that they are the expert and you don't really know what you're talking about. If that happens, you must never be defensive or you get into the pantomime routine of, "Yes it is, no it isn't." Instead, try and find out what they really think and then use the phrase, "Yes, and…" Never ever say, "Yes, but…" The "but" indicates that you're counter-attacking them rather than acknowledging their expertise.

Perhaps someone picks on the weakest part of your argument or pitch and ridicules it. They imply that, because that part is wrong, everything else you've said must be rubbish. Again, don't allow yourself to get riled and don't give up hope. Simply acknowledge their point and tell them that you'll check it, or ask them what they would suggest instead. Then take back control and return to the rest of your pitch.

" ARGUMENT IS THE WORST SORT OF CONVERSATION "

JONATHAN SWIFT (1667–1745), ANGLO-IRISH ESSAYIST

IN PETER JONES'S QUIZZING OF TECH 21'S JASON ROBERTS *(see pp204–5), he ridiculed Jason's valuation of his company (based on the equity he was offering in relation to the investment he sought). Yet, despite this, Peter ended up making Jason an offer and the two eventually negotiated a deal! Indeed the scorn poured on Jason's valuation could even be seen as a tactic in Peter's negotiating arsenal to put the entrepreneur on the back foot and soften him up for the kind of high equity deal Peter wanted to achieve.*

The main thing to remember if you are faced with challenging questions is to avoid becoming defensive and argumentative. And definitely don't respond with a counter-attack!

CONCLUSION

We will reiterate that questions are a key opportunity for you to show off your knowledge, build your credibility and gauge the interest of the audience. Don't be frightened of them; instead, use them to your advantage. Always do your preparation and follow the seven simple steps outlined in this Commandment so you connect with the audience and demonstrate your confidence.

PHYSICOOL

THE PHYSICOOL BANDAGE *is pre-packed ready for use; it can be re-used, however, with a coolant top-up spray.*

Kay Russell went into the Den looking for investment in Physicool, a business retailing reusable cooling bandages for muscle injuries. Kay's was a very natural presentation, mixing hiccups such as forgetting to state what the Physicool product was with a good head for figures and an honest, open response to the Dragons' questions.

The questioning was wide ranging and pointed at times. Impressively, Kay kept an even keel throughout, even when Peter Jones expressed concerns about the fact that Kay had set up a separate company in which she was seeking investment, when she already had a similar and profitable company focused on the equine market. 'Market' was key to Kay's response, as she explained that the equine market was for race and top-level eventing horses and, therefore, a very small and specialist market. Whereas, with the separately branded Physicool, she was looking towards a much wider sports and health market, and this was the market that had potential for sales growth and, therefore, investment.

There was something refreshing about Kay's performance. She was engaging without seeming forced, and the way in which she answered questions was solid and straightforward without sounding rehearsed. It's achieved only by thoroughly knowing your business and product.

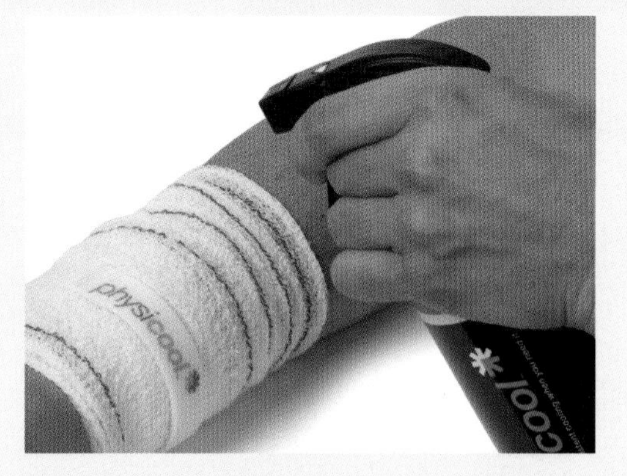

IN SPRING 2010 *Physicool launched in 800 branches of Boots across the UK. As well as the sports market, it is being used widely in the healthcare sector.*

KAY UNDERWENT THE USUAL BARRAGE OF QUESTIONS *over her projected sales figures plus a further inquisition over her existing equine-based company. She coped with the questioning well, and Kay's tilted head posture is a telling signal that she's listening to and considering the questions; it also suggests empathy, especially when smiling or laughing. Deborah appreciated the need to have the two businesses branded differently, and so was happy to invest.*

COMMANDMENT 7

USE YOUR VOICE

Are you ready to make this your first and best tool?

THE THREE THINGS that best demonstrate passion are how you handle your props, how you look (your body language) and how you sound. And in some ways your voice is the most important of them all. You'll be using your voice to deliver your speech and answer questions. Every nuance of your voice, every variation in pitch and tone, every point of emphasis and also every pause will count. Use the tips in this chapter to train your voice, get over the ubiquitous barriers of dry mouth and loss of breath, and talk with confidence.

WHY YOU NEED TO WORK ON YOUR VOICE

The voice alone conjures up images. This is obvious when you take a phone call from a stranger. Within seconds you will start to build a mental picture of the individual at the other end of the line. Perhaps the telesales person sounds flirty and fun-loving, so you picture them as someone young and fresh-faced. In reality, of course, they could be much older and grizzly. Even when you're face-to-face with a stranger, the moment they open their mouth you start to change your perception about their whole persona. A weak or monotonous voice makes for a weak or monotonous presentation.

You don't need a powerful voice to speak to a small group, but you do need to take care of it and learn how to control it.

When you start your presentation the audience expects you to be a bit nervous and you'll find that your voice will probably quiver. Don't worry about this. In fact a small amount of stage fright is actually quite good because it gets you on your toes and makes you produce cortisol, the adrenaline of the brain. On the other hand, you don't want your voice to act completely against you during your presentation, which is why you should prepare your voice just as much as you should prepare your notes and props.

FIVE TIPS FOR A BETTER VOICE

Here's a summary of five important points about the voice, which we will be covering in this Commandment.

1. Treat your voice with respect – like an instrument – and don't abuse or overuse it.

2 Learn to breathe deep and low into your tummy, not into your chest. You can start practising the breathing exercises in this Commandment today.

3 Always warm up your voice before you use it in earnest. Get over feelings of self-consciousness about doing warming up exercises.

4 Learn how to control the pitch, pace and modulation of your voice so you can bewitch the audience.

5 Develop different styles of voice to engage with the audience at the right moment. You will be practising by reading something out aloud in each of your different voices.

PAUL TINTON *gave a great pitch for Prowaste (see p61). He spoke with the confidence of someone experienced in presenting business proposals. He also spoke to the Dragons as equals and dealt with a wide range of questions in a composed manner. Paul's advice is to "think long and hard about who you are talking to … What makes them tick? Where have they been successful in the past? What factors aided that success? I drafted the pitch with that in mind, to try and anchor their interest in our company."*

" REGARD YOUR VOICE AS CAPITAL IN THE BANK. SING ON YOUR INTEREST AND YOUR VOICE WILL LAST. "

LAURITZ MELCHIOR (1890–1973), DANISH-BORN OPERA SINGER

RESPECT YOUR VOICE

The voice is a complex and delicate instrument that most of us ignore. In fact to speak we have to use our brain, our breath and our voice box. It's only professional singers and stage actors who nurture and regularly exercise their voices. When the rest of us speak we just let it happen.

As a general point, if you find that your voice becomes strained while you are giving your presentation, it's because you're not breathing properly and trying to say things without enough air. Stop doing it, check your breathing and continue at a slower pace. Nobody's going to worry if you need to take a sip of water.

During a presentation, it's probably best to speak slower than you would normally. When we start to give a presentation we automatically speed up because we want to finish as soon as possible. The answer is to slow down so you can concentrate on pronouncing every word, and finishing each thought before you go on to the next. When you practise regularly you will find the right speed that allows you to think of the context, remember the content and to control your own voice.

SAMANTHA GORE AND HER SABOTEUR CRIME PREVENTION PRODUCTS *crashed and burned in the Den in Series 6. Breathing fast, she launched into her presentation, nervous energy fizzing from her. Her voice became tight and strained, her expressions often full of angst. Unfortunately, despite practising over and over again beforehand, the pitch lost direction and focus. Samantha was, as Theo described her, "an enigma". Indeed she was: Samantha was a proven entrepreneur, who ran a successful Japanese restaurant in Manchester, had helped other start-up businesses and written a couple of books. She had an ability for electronic inventions, yet the Dragons found it hard to assess the products she brought to the Den as they were surrounded by a fog of confusion in the way Samantha talked about them and described their genesis. As Theo continued: "You're obviously academically brilliant, you're successful in business already, you've got some great ideas … but you're unfocused." Duncan's summation was briefer: "I don't know whether you're completely bonkers or a complete and utter genius."*

When giving a presentation, never try and talk over loud noises such as aircraft, trains or pneumatic drills. And generally, when you're in a noisy and crowded room talk into the noise rather than trying to talk above or below it.

SOME POINTS ABOUT FOOD AND DRINK

What you eat and drink can have a direct effect on the voice. Bear in mind these points.

- **DAIRY PRODUCTS.** Try and avoid dairy products in the days leading up to your pitch as they will produce mucus. There's nothing worse than having to clear your throat continuously during a presentation.

- **PRE-PITCH MEAL.** You don't want to have to compete with a grumbling stomach, so eat something light a couple of hours before your pitch. You may be nervous and not feeling hungry, but you should have a nutritious snack.

- **CAFFEINE AND ALCOHOL.** Yes, caffeine might give you energy and a buzz in the head, and alcohol might make you feel more relaxed, but don't have alcohol or loads of coffee before you speak. They dry out your voice and make you sound hoarse.

- **WATER.** Your voice needs lubricating, and the very best liquid for it is water. Drink it at room temperature – without ice. Your voice doesn't need cooling.

LEVI ROOTS

Levi Roots famously used his voice and guitar to serenade the Dragons back in Series 4, ascending the stairs while strumming a tune and singing the praises of his Reggae Reggae jerk barbecue sauce. Despite getting his figures spectacularly wrong on the programme, he used his mellifluous tones to extol the virtues of his sauce – rather like Goldilocks's porridge it was neither too hot nor too insipid – and gave his back story, working as a musician and selling this home-recipe sauce at every Notting Hill Carnival for years.

Richard Farleigh and Peter Jones invested in Levi's Reggae Reggae Sauce, and since then both the sauce and the man have gone from strength to strength. The sauce is now sold extensively throughout the UK, the range having been developed to include further sauces and spiced nuts, and Levi has written a bestselling book on Caribbean cuisine.

LEVI *has continued with his musicianship too, releasing the album 'Red Hot' in 2009.*

PAUL WARD OF PARAGON PE *appeared in Series 7 and gave an assured but curiously low-key presentation that served to distance himself from the Dragons. His company had already been trading successfully for three years, selling antimicrobial cleaning products, and that obviously gave Paul confidence in his position. His calm demeanor and unanimated delivery, though, gave the impression that he was equivocal about gaining a Dragon's investment – that he could take it or leave it. Given the success of his business then and its upward trajectory since, that may well have been the case. James Caan eventually did make what seemed to be a reasonable offer, but after a few moments of reflection Paul turned it down and left the Den empty-handed.*

BREATHING EXERCISES

When the doctor says "take a deep breath" we naturally pull our tummy in and suck air into our chest. This is called an upper chest breath and it's fine if the doctor wants to check out your lungs, but it's not good for speaking.

You need to take low breaths using your diaphragm to suck the air deep down into your belly. This is called a low-deep breath. We all know that your lungs aren't down there, but when you use the diaphragm to breathe it looks and feels like the air is going down into your tummy. It slows you down and calms you. It will also make you sound knowledgeable, confident and in control.

- **LIE ON YOUR BACK.** Try it out by lying on the floor, on your back with one hand on your tummy just below the belly button and the other hand on your chest.

"WORDS MEAN MORE THAN WHAT IS SET DOWN ON PAPER. IT TAKES THE HUMAN VOICE TO INFUSE THEM WITH SHADES OF DEEPER MEANING."

MAYA ANGELOU, AMERICAN AUTHOR

- **BREATHE THROUGH THE NOSE.** Pull up your diaphragm and breathe slowly out through your nose. You should feel your tummy deflate.

- **BREATHE THROUGH THE MOUTH.** Now breathe in through your mouth and pull the air down into your stomach. You should feel your tummy expand and your chest remain still. Repeat this a few times using your mouth.

- **BREATHE SLOWLY AND STEADILY.** Your breathing should now be slow and smooth and you should feel relaxed. You're probably doing about four or five breaths per minute. Stay here for a few more minutes.

- **DO IT STANDING.** When you're happy, try standing up. Start by inhaling through your nose and exhaling through your mouth. Then use your mouth rather than your nose.

SHARON WRIGHT OF MAGNAMOLE
(see pp34–5) gave some useful insight into how she prepared to speak in the Den: "I practised every day for three weeks, talking into a dictaphone after jogging up and down my office corridor – it prepares your lungs for talking under pressure because adrenaline is a crusher and you have no control over the release of the chemical."

This is how you should breathe when you do your presentation, but obviously not with your hand on your stomach. It will feel uncomfortable at first, but if you keep practising the breathing exercises it will become more natural.

A good idea is to practise every morning in the bathroom, after you've brushed your teeth and before you get going for the day, and again at night, before you go to bed.

WARM-UP EXERCISES

Like any instrument the voice needs to warm up before you start to use it seriously. You wouldn't turn the ignition key on a Formula 1 racing car and go immediately into the race. You'd warm up the engine to thin the oil and loosen the bearings. It's the same for your voice when you're about to do a presentation or speech.

Remember nobody expects you to be perfect. But if you breathe properly and warm up your voice before you start, you'll be much

" LOWER YOUR VOICE AND STRENGTHEN YOUR ARGUMENT "

LEBANESE PROVERB

more relaxed and look and sound much more confident. You'll also reduce the risk of straining your voice.

This is what to do:

- **CALM DOWN YOUR BREATHING.** Take three or four slow, low-deep breaths and feel yourself relax. The key word is slow as it will calm you down. It will take you about a minute.

- **EXERCISE THE MUSCLES OF YOUR MOUTH AND TONGUE.** Get your mouth moving by yawning and opening it very wide. Rub your lips together as though you were a woman spreading your lipstick. Stick out your tongue as far as it'll go and try to lick your chin and then your nose. Do this a couple of times and then say, "Tut, tut, tut" a few times using your tongue against the roof of your mouth.

- **EXERCISE YOUR LARYNX.** Warm up your larynx with a few tongue-twisters. Some good ones are, "The two twenty train tore through the tunnel" and, "Red lorry, yellow lorry". Say them each two or three times, getting faster and faster as you do it.

AVOID THE MONOTONE

How do you think it sounds when someone reads something out aloud in a dry monotone voice? You'll think it's boring and you'll probably switch off. It's just like one of those statements read out by lawyers where "Lessons will be learnt". You know in your heart that they don't mean it because there's no passion or enthusiasm in their voice. Words on their own just convey content, whereas the way the speaker delivers them convey the emotion and what the speaker feels about them.

GET THE PACE RIGHT

Pace is how fast you speak. If you go too fast, the audience will struggle to keep up and won't take it all in. Next time you hear a radio advert for a car, try and make out the bit about credit terms that they're talking about at the end. It's the verbal equivalent of the small print and deliberately speeded up so you can't understand it. If you speak too slowly, the audience will struggle to keep awake and think you're boring and maybe a bit patronizing.

You need to use a pace that has energy, but is easy for people to follow what you're talking about. You also need to vary it so people stay awake and are interested in what you're saying. There's nothing worse than sounding monotonous. So speed up to show enthusiasm and slow down to be thoughtful.

Listen to the news on the radio or television and hear how the presenters vary their voice according to the content. You must learn to do the same. Practise by reading a piece from one of the tabloid newspapers out loud. The tabloids are easy because they use short simple sentences that are almost like the way we speak.

During your pitch, when you first stand up to speak you're bound to be nervous. As a consequence, you're likely to start speaking faster than normal. So to compensate for that natural nervous reaction you must deliberately slow down even more than your normal pace. You'll find that as you calm down, after a minute or so your voice will return to its usual speed.

VICTORIA MCGRANE OF NEUROTICA *appeared in the Den in Series 6. The pitch started well but began to unravel over the finances and costs of producing a fashion range. None of the Dragons felt that Victoria was asking for enough money to make a go of it. Victoria's voice remained calm and even, though, and she remained confident that she could achieve her immediate objectives on the budget she had set. Her composure stood her in good stead, even as three of the Dragons ruled themselves out in quick succession, and Peter eventually decided that he would offer Victoria a larger investment of £75,000.*

BUILD IN PAUSES

As mentioned before, you should pause now and then to grab the audience's attention. A short pause is less than a second. A longer pause, of a second or two, becomes a stop and gives the audience time to catch up. You pause after a word or phrase to give them a chance to take it in. Or pause before a word to grab their attention and get them on the edge of their seats waiting for your next word. Great speakers like Winston Churchill were masters of the pause, and comedians use the pregnant pause just before the punch line to generate the laugh.

LESLEY-ANN SIMMONS *used her nervous energy to her advantage when she went into the Den to pitch for her franchise business Shoes Galore in Series 6. With a naturally jolly disposition, Lesley-Ann peppered her pitch with spontaneous bursts of laughter and giggles. While this isn't a ploy that one would generally advise for business pitches, in Lesley-Ann's case it was so natural, so irrepressibly part of her character, that it charmed and rather disarmed the Dragons. Of course, investment isn't all laughs, and Lesley-Ann was adept with her business plan and figures too, and so presented well overall. She didn't get the investment she went for though, as the Dragons feared the amount of capital she would be putting into stock to supply the new franchisees she intended to recruit. It was advice that Lesley-Ann heeded, and she subsequently sold the business in order to seek out and start up her next entrepreneurial venture.*

PLAY WITH PITCH

In Western society a low deep voice signals authority and strength, and a high pitch portrays youth and excitement. This is true for both men and women. So when you talk about facts you should lower your voice to appear self-assured, knowledgeable and confident. By contrast, when you talk about your product or sales, you should speak slightly higher to show energy and enthusiasm.

If you do the breathing exercises that we mentioned earlier in this chapter, your voice will become deeper and your vocal range broader. Another way to train your voice to sound deeper is to sing along to some music but in an octave lower than the performer.

When you start your presentation your nerves will cause you throat muscles naturally to constrict. This will make your voice sound higher so speak a bit deeper when you start. But if you do the breathing exercises before you speak, your voice will sound normal.

USE INFLECTION BEFORE A PAUSE

If you drop the pitch of your voice just before a pause, the audience will think you've finished a sentence. You need to speak like the Australians do at the end of a sentence and raise the pitch of your voice on the word before the pause. This will create anticipation and suspense. Then pause before you use the same pitch on the word after the pause.

PUNCH UP THE VOLUME

You can also make individual words and phrases stand out by saying them slightly louder. It's like using a highlighter pen to emphasize written words. Similarly you will draw the audience in if you speak some words slightly quieter, as though you're sharing a secret.

" YOUR VOICE IS A MUSCLE AND YOU HAVE TO TRAIN IT JUST LIKE AN ATHLETE TRAINS ANY ONE OF THEIR MUSCLES "

GARY DEGRAIDE, AMERICAN BROADCASTER

DEVELOP DIFFERENT VOICES

We all have a natural way that we speak for most of the time – our normal voice. Most of us put on a different voice when we talk to our boss, our parents and our children. What we do without realizing is change the pitch, the pace, the tone and the volume briefly to connect with the person who's listening. We do it when we go from one role to another and it has a subconscious effect on the listener. It's like putting a label on what you're going to talk about.

Develop the following voices for different parts of your presentation:

- **YOUR 'NORMAL' VOICE.** Your 'normal' voice is the one you would use when having an intimate conversation with just one person who has the same status as you. You don't want to sound as though you're talking down to your audience. You must talk to them on a more personal level, and one way is to focus on one person in the audience at a time, as though they were a close friend, moving on to another after a few seconds.

- **YOUR FACTUAL VOICE.** This voice is lower and flatter than your normal voice, which makes you sound knowledgeable, authoritative and self-assured. It's not too slow but almost monotone, and you should use it when you're talking about facts and figures such as market share and costs. You shouldn't use it, however, when you talk about projected sales figures – use an enthusiastic voice for them.

- **YOUR ENTHUSIASTIC VOICE.** Reserve your most upbeat, optimistic voice for your product or service itself.

- **YOUR SERIOUS VOICE.** This is also slow and deep. But it's precise and full of short pauses as though you're very carefully choosing your words. You will use it towards the end of your presentation, when you're talking about the investment. You might also use it during the question and answer session and during any negotiation.

- **YOUR STORY VOICE.** Make this warm, friendly and soft with lots of changes of pitch and tone. You will use it when you're telling your 'war stories' and other anecdotes. You might also move slightly nearer the audience and speak slightly quieter as it makes them feel a bit more intimate with you.

Practise your different voices by reading out loud at about 100 words a minute. Read something like an article from the business section of a newspaper for your factual and serious voices. A children's story such as *Winnie the Pooh* will help you develop your story voice, and an item from a tabloid newspaper or modern novel should help with your normal and enthusiastic voices.

In summary, your voice is one of your most important assets and you need to learn how to use it and respect it. It's how you connect with the audience on an emotional level and draw them into your pitch.

CASE STUDY **FROM SERIES 6 EPISODE 4**

THE OLIVE MAN

When Michael North pitched an idea to the Dragons for a members-only club for receiving fresh, seasonal olive oil, it offered a great example of a presentation that really fired enthusiasm about the subject. Michael's voice was dynamic, rising and falling, slowing down and speeding up, stressing words, repeating phrases and asking rhetorical questions ("Guess what?" "Why, why, why would you want to invest?") to emphasize his points. There was a seductive rhythm to his speech too and his vocabulary was rich with descriptions, such as the aroma of an oil that he likened to "wet fields of hay". Keen to educate about both the wonders and misconceptions of olive oil, he was also ready to argue and contradict the Dragons in matters of taste and knowledge – with just enough charm to get away with it. In his element when talking about the product, Michael also furnished

MICHAEL'S ENGAGING STYLE *and way with words allowed the Dragons to enjoy his pitch.*

each of the Dragons with a small taster of fresh olive oil. Following his tutored tasting, they first warmed the cups of oil in their hands, then gave it a good nose, before tasting the oil. As they did so, his voice accelerated to the speed of a motor racing commentary: "Here we go. It's a roller-coaster... we've got rocket, we've got sorrel... we've got rising bitterness. Whack! Here comes a pepper kick..."

It was theatrical, entertaining stuff, and, as Deborah Meaden commented, Michael was clearly "a man of superlatives". Okay, ultimately none of the Dragons went for Michael's deal – each concluding that this was more of a lifestyle business than one they could invest in – but Michael's engaging style allowed the Dragons to appreciate the raison d'être of the business.

MICHAEL LED THE DRAGONS *in a connoisseur's olive oil tasting. Describing the flavours and sensations with a rich vocabulary, he wanted to create a sense of appreciation, even reverence, for quality olive oil that's seasonal and fresh.*

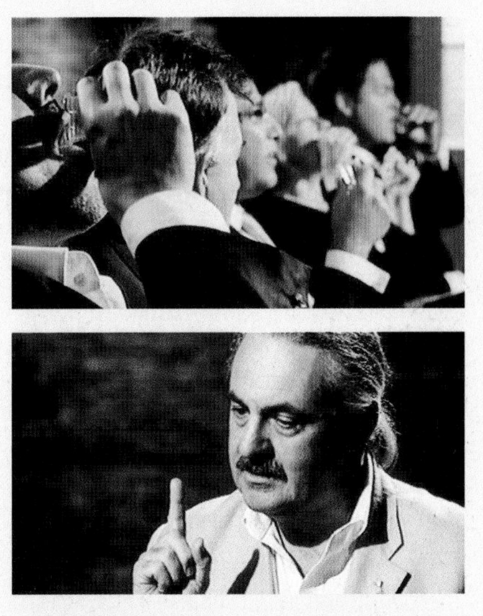

WHILE EXPOUNDING *on the cascade of tastes emanating from the oil, Michael suddenly paused, with finger held aloft, to emphasize a key point – that fresh olive oil leaves no greasy residue in the mouth.*

COMMANDMENT 8

TALK WITH YOUR BODY

Can you use your body language
to reinforce your message?

AS YOU WALK INTO THE ROOM, and before you even open your mouth, the audience will have made a judgement about you. We can all tell so much about a person from the way they dress and how they carry themselves. Instinctively we read the signals that tell us what they feel about themselves, the situation they're in at the moment, and their status. Try watching an episode of Dragons' Den with the sound turned down. What is your impression of each new participant within seconds of them entering the Den? And what are they saying with their bodies as they deliver their pitch? Also keep an eye on the body language of the Dragons themselves as they listen to the pitch – are they looking attentive, bored, curious, baffled, astonished?

BODY LANGUAGE – A PRIMER

Research suggests that 55% of our first impression of someone comes simply from how the person looks. How you dress and how you stand count for more than what you actually say, and that first impression takes a long time to change.

When you stand there and do your pitch your audience will subconsciously give out signals that show you what they are thinking. We call this non-verbal communications or body language. The source of this communication may seem a bit mystical until you realize that in primeval times the ability to 'read' what the other person was thinking or intended to do was a matter of survival.

In the days of the silent movies actors like Buster Keaton and Charlie Chaplin learnt how to talk with their body. After all, gestures, postures and facial expressions were the only way they had to communicate with the audience. They were masters at it.

> **" THE MOVEMENTS OF EXPRESSION REVEAL OUR THOUGHTS AND INTENTIONS MORE TRULY THAN OUR WORDS, WHICH CAN BE FALSIFIED "**
>
> CHARLES DARWIN

Body language as a science dates back over 350 years when John Bulwer produced a book called *Chirologia – The Natural Language of the Hand*. This was published in 1644 and described the various hand movements and gestures that humans use to communicate.

Charles Darwin produced the most influential work with his book called *The Expressions of Emotions in Man and Animals*, which was published in 1872.

Then in the 1950s an American anthropologist, Ray Birdwhistell, used slow motion film to analyse people's body movements, postures and facial expressions. He worked out that we use and recognize thousands of facial expressions, and he published his findings as *An Introduction to Kinesics* in 1952.

These days we classify body language into three groups.

- **SIGNALS WE USE INSTEAD OF SPEECH.** These are simple things like the thumbs-up sign or a nod of the head, which are obvious to most people in the Western world.

- **GESTURES THAT REINFORCE WHAT WE'RE SAYING.** We all use our arms, hands and facial expressions to add further meaning to what we're talking about. In this chapter we will look at how to interpret these gestures and harness them when you give your pitch.

- **SIGNS THAT REFLECT OUR MOOD AND THOUGHTS.** Without realizing it, all of us automatically signal our mood and what we're thinking with our hands and face. After all, we all understand the meaning of a smile or a frown. Some signs are more subtle, though, and we'll look at them in this chapter, too.

It's almost impossible to tell what someone is thinking from a photograph. You must always decode body language from a *cluster* of different signals or a movement from one sign to another. You have to do this in the context of what is going on around them.

Take arm-folding, for example. If someone has folded their arms, it could just be that they are cold. However, if they fold their arms when you start to talk to them, they are being defensive or they are rejecting what you said. Similarly if they unfold their arms when you talk to them, they are accepting you and receptive to what you are talking about.

Folded arms are called a 'closed posture', and other closed forms are looking down, turning slightly away and, if you're a man, holding your hands in front of your genitals.

When you give your pitch you have to watch the audience and notice their body language. If the majority give out the same non-verbal messages, then you might have to change what you're doing, what you're saying and how you're speaking.

IS YOUR AUDIENCE BORED OR ATTENTIVE?

There are many signs that tell you people are bored. Yawning, heads drooping and eyes closing are probably the most obvious! Other fairly conspicuous signs would be when they start to look around the room or out of the window. Or they might glance at their watch or doodle on their pad. If that's what most of the audience are doing, you need to move on to the next topic. Sometimes this is difficult and is another reason why PowerPoint (see pp107–8) is not the best visual medium. If you use slides it's not always easy to skip forwards without appearing to gloss over or dismiss a topic out of hand.

Similarly, someone shuffling in their seat means they're restless. And fast movements such as drumming their fingers on the chair or table, twiddling their thumbs or tapping their feet mean that they are impatient and want you to hurry up. In that case you must get straight to the point and move on as soon as possible.

Another less obvious sign is when someone is sitting with their chin resting on the palm of their hand. The rule of thumb is that if the weight of their head is on their hand, they are bored.

In the same way if they lean back in their chair, they are probably not interested in what you are talking about. It's a sign that they want to move away from you. And if you see them stretch out their legs at the same time and stare at the ceiling, you have completely lost them!

On the other side of the coin, if they look at you and lean slightly forwards as you speak, they are paying attention. They might also

DRAGON DUNCAN BANNATYNE *tends to lean to one side in his seat with a hand raised to his face when he is analysing the pitch of an entrepreneur in the Den. If Duncan makes up his mind that he doesn't like the pitch, however, he is quick to show it by looking around distractedly and perhaps even scowling in displeasure.*

JAMES CAAN *is the poker player in the Den – the Dragon that gives away the least with his body language. He sits back, speaks calmly throughout and strokes his beard a lot when deliberating. He often fixes the entrepreneur with his gaze at such times, but occasionally he'll look skywards instead, as if weighing up the pros and cons of what's being offered. Involuntary emotions, such as smiles and laughter, he tends to hide or keep to himself, lowering his head or even raising hands to disguise his emotions – all to maintain the controlled, poker face attitude.*

tilt their head slightly to one side or nod now and then to show that they are interested in what you are talking about. But be careful about how you interpret head movements, as a prolonged nod usually means "Yes, but...".

If you see the audience starting to show signs of boredom, try putting more life into your voice. Or you could ask them if they have any questions at that point. That usually wakes them up!

WHAT DO THEY THINK OF YOUR PITCH?

Most people will naturally touch their face with their fingers as they consider what they're seeing and hearing. They will then make a decision, and their body language might tell you whether they agree or disagree with your argument or proposition.

So while people evaluate what you are talking about during your presentation they will lean back slightly in the chair as though they are thinking and put their hand to their cheek. You will see that their forefinger and thumb will point up and the rest of their fingers will be curled around into their palm. This is known as the 'positive evaluation posture'. In other words they are interested in what you are saying and are thinking about it in a positive light.

The complete opposite is when they adopt the 'negative evaluation posture'. In this case their chin will rest on their thumb with their head slightly tilted down. It tells you fairly clearly that they disagree or don't approve of what you are saying.

PETER JONES *demonstrates an agile mind in the Den – he's the Dragon who can most rapidly flip from light to dark or vice versa. His expression tends to be rather stern when he's concentrating and this can intensify when he's quizzing an entrepreneur. But he's capable of changing mood quickly. When cogitating deeply, he tends to hang his head to one side and hide his face behind a hand drawn up to his brow.*

When they are about to make a decision, most people will stroke their chin with their thumb and forefinger. So if somebody in the audience strokes their chin when you are going through some of the detail in your pitch and then leans back and folds their arms, they have most likely rejected your idea. However if they stroke their chin and then lean slightly forward with their head up, they have accepted it. Remember that the best way to interpret body language signals is to look at a cluster or sequence of movements and not read too much into a single sign or gesture.

People will often nod or shake their head as they think about what you are saying. A quick nod is a positive agreement, but a prolonged nod probably means they don't agree with everything that you've said. A shake of the head means "No", and when the shake is repeated in quick succession it means "No way". If this is the case they will often mutter under their breath at the same time.

When you stand there giving your pitch you must keep an eye on the Decision Makers in the audience. If they appear to disagree or reject your ideas you may want to raise the issue at that point. For instance you could say something along the lines of, "You seemed slightly concerned with that...", then wait for their response before you continue.

WHAT DO THEY FEEL?

You must pay particular attention to people's hands during the question and answer session or when you're negotiating. This is when they will signal how they feel about their position. The most common signal that they give when they are pleased with themselves is to hold their hands together so just their fingertips touch. This is

DEBORAH MEADEN'S *body language is very telling, not least in the combination of facial expressions and hand gestures. She uses her hands to almost draw the answers out of entrepreneurs at times, locking in on them with her eyes and forcing them to concentrate on the information she's after. She's like a film director. She'll also use a raised hand to stop someone mid-track, if she wants to interject or disagree with what they're saying. If Deborah's holding a pen, two fingers raised emphatically have the same effect. In negotiations, sometimes she'll raise a finger up to her mouth when she doesn't want to negotiate any more. At this point, it's usually a simple yes or no for the deal.*

THE SEQUENCE SHOWN TO RIGHT *is when Michael North (see pp160–1) told Deborah that she had never tasted really good fresh olive oil so wasn't in a position to judge whether supermarket olive oil was good or bad. The implication of Deborah's final gesture, with a fist raised to her mouth, is emphatic, and if Michael were to have somehow transformed into an irksome fly crawling across the table at that point, he would probably have been pulverized to oblivion …*

THEO PAPHITIS, *of all the Dragons, is the most open and expressive with his face. He never bothers to hide anything, and there's always a drama unfolding across his face, as he furrows his brow in puzzlement, raises one eyebrow in incredulity, offers a big grin when he's happy, and shouts out for what he wants like a fan at a football match. He does nothing to hide his emotions – even moments of uncertainty – so the entrepreneur shouldn't be in any doubt about whether their pitch is going well or badly with Theo. All of this openness, however, doesn't make him any easier to negotiate with. He happily occupies the throne-like middle position with the high-backed chair, and there's something, if not quite regal, then certainly Don-like in the way that he'll offer a deal – as if to say, "It's a favour I'm offering, and you'd be very silly to quibble."*

called 'the steeple', and the higher the steeple points the more pleased they are with themselves and the position they're in. If you play chess with someone and you see them do a high steeple with their elbows on the table, you know that they think they will check-mate you within a couple of moves. Similarly if they steeple their hands when you are negotiating, they are pretty sure that they have won.

If they wring their hands, it means that they feel anxious. If they clench them together with their fingers intertwined, they feel frustrated. But rubbing their palms together is a positive sign. If they rub quickly, they are excited about both of you doing well. However, if they rub them slowly, it's for their own benefit.

Finally there are a couple of gestures that people do with their hands and arms together. When they plead for an agreement they will often do a 'begging gesture' with both palms upwards. When they want to take things steady they might do a 'slowing down gesture' with both palms facing down.

OBSERVING BODY LANGUAGE

You should try and learn how to 'read' people in general well before you go in to deliver your pitch. The best way to do this is to watch and observe people in a group. A good time and place is early evening in a bar near the commercial centre of any town. Sit in a corner and watch the groups of accountants and solicitors come in to unwind after work. Try and work out what they are talking about and who's the alpha male/female and who is the beta male/female. Then the trick you have to achieve during your pitch is to observe your audience when you talk, interpret the signs that tell you what they feel and adjust your pitch accordingly.

GET YOUR CLOTHING RIGHT

You always need to dress to conform to the situation you're in. When you meet a potential investor, or even the Dragons themselves, you should therefore be in a suit, but making sure that yours doesn't outshine theirs. A £1,500 silk suit from Armani would probably be over the top for a man, as would be an all-red power suit for a woman. You need to look confident but not arrogant; successful but not extravagant.

" DRESSING LIKE THAT CERTAINLY DOESN'T APPEAL TO ME. SO FIRST OFF, YOU'VE ALREADY INSTANTLY GOT MY BACK UP. "

PETER JONES, DRAGON

LEARN HOW TO MAKE A GOOD ENTRANCE

How you dress is only part of the story. How you come into the room, how you carry yourself and what you do when you meet them are other factors that will make an impression on your audience. You must come across as believable and professional. This will establish your credibility, inspire their confidence and influence their decision.

There are three elements to making a good entrance, which in essence are calmness, posture, and greeting. We'll look at them here and also put them into context in Commandment 10, which covers the order of events on the actual day of your pitch.

CALMNESS

You want to carry an aura of calmness with your entrance. Ideally that will mean taking a deep breath as you stand at the threshold, stepping into the room then stopping to look around and greeting the audience. You will be nervous and liable to rushing, but you need to learn to slow down. What sort of impression would it give if you hurry in with papers and equipment in your arms?

POSTURE

Adopt a posture for your entrance so you stand tall, and look relaxed and confident. Roll your shoulders back to stop them sagging, stretch your neck and raise your head so you look ahead, not at the floor. Take your hands out of your pockets when you first meet someone – they need to feel that you're not hiding something in your hands. (Which historically is one of the reasons we all shake hands.) It's not just for the sake of your audience that you want to have a good posture – the taller you stand, the more confident you will feel.

GREETING

Your handshake and how you say "hello" will tell the other person how you feel about yourself and what you think about them. A proper handshake is easy. You face them and look them in the eyes (or at their face if you prefer). Hold out your hand so you'll shake with your palms together. Smile and say "hello" with a nice warm and friendly voice. You'll then come across as confident, relaxed and pleased to meet them.

Do not let them intimidate you. Just because they might have your future in their hands, remember they're only human.

HANDSHAKES TO AVOID

- The **WET FISH** feels exactly as it sounds. Limp and with the fingers rather than the palm. It says "I'm uncomfortable meeting you and don't feel good about myself." In other words you have low self-esteem and lack confidence. You must not do it.

- The **BONE-CRUNCHER** is very unpleasant and sometimes can be painful. It's generally done by men who want to show how strong and powerful they are. But they're usually the opposite. Someone who's powerful has a certain aura and doesn't need to show off with the bone cruncher. You must not do it as you are looking for a partnership.

- The **OVER-HANDER** is another dominant handshake. It's where you twist the palm of your hand horizontal as you start to shake hands so their hand is underneath yours. It sends the message that you feel superior to them and they're beneath you, whether that's your intention or not. It's not very nice as it will make them feel uncomfortable.

WHY NON-VERBAL COMMUNICATION IS IMPORTANT

Words work on the brain. They are succinct and good at getting across concrete ideas and facts. To convey feelings is much more difficult with just words. Although a good author can conjure up images in the reader's mind fairly easily, most of us can't.

CASE STUDY **FROM SERIES 7 EPISODE 5**

JANE RAFTER

You can learn a lot about body language by watching Dragons' Den. Controlling one's body language is hard enough during a pitch, let alone in front of the cameras. However, some people are naturally more at ease in this environment than others. Such was the case with Jane Rafter, who went into the Den to pitch for her innovative sandals business, Slinks.

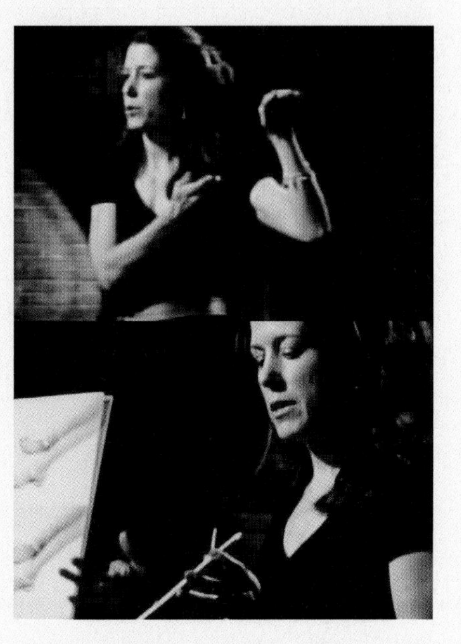

JANE *used her hands expressively to demonstrate how she wanted her sandals displayed in shops and to pinpoint details of the sandal's design.*

Jane looked relaxed and comfortable in front of the Dragons, engaging them with gestures as she demonstrated her products. Jane was especially expressive with her hands, holding one to her heart to emphasize the point that she knew that women loved these shoes. She was also very dexterous in the way that she presented the delicate sandals. As with the case of Motormouse (see pp186–7), because the items were small, it made sense for Jane to dress simply and in black to better showcase the products she was holding.

Non-verbal communications or body language works on instinct. We take it on board as a feeling rather than as a logical thought. This is why we often feel someone is lying to us, but we don't know why. It's all about postures, gestures and movements which are involuntary and are done without the other person knowing.

So during your presentation the audience will hear your words and look at your visuals. They will instinctively know how you feel about it from the way you stand and how you move your body. They'll be able to tell when you're unsure of your facts or uncertain about your sales figures.

When you give your presentation you must look confident, but also relaxed. A small amount of nerves are okay when you first stand up because the audience expect them, and they make you alert. But nerves are not a good sign when you're in full flight, particularly when you're talking about sales and costs. If you look too nervous the audience will subconsciously feel that you're hiding something, or not being totally honest.

SIGNS OF NERVES AND HOW TO SUPPRESS THEM

The problem with body language is that it's instinctive and comes from within you. But you can control some of your nerves by feeling confident, relaxed and good about yourself and your pitch. And you can eliminate most of the signs of nerves with a few simple techniques.

For instance if you pick up a pen when you're giving your presentation and you're nervous in any way, you will play with it. How many times have you seen the presenter twirling a pen through their fingers or tossing it from one hand to the next? That's easy to control. Some are more difficult and they all fall into one of four groups – physiological, fiddles, fidgets and fillers.

- **PHYSIOLOGICAL FACTORS.** Things like sweating, dry mouth, quivering voice and shaking knees are very difficult to control and you just have to cope with them. So, for instance, if your mouth is dry, take a sip of water. We will look at some of the things you can do to reduce these in Commandments 9 and 10.

- **FIDDLING WITH OBJECTS.** Guys, don't put your hands in your pockets, or you'll play with your keys or coins. Women, leave your hair alone. Don't pick up a pen or pointer unless you're going to use it. When you've finished, put it down. The same with your props. Try to avoid even putting your hands together because, if you're in any way nervous, you will probably automatically start playing with your rings or fiddling with your fingers themselves.

- **FIDGETING.** Fidgeting happens subconsciously when you don't have any objects to fiddle with, for example, if you're standing, you might start shifting your weight from one foot to the other. When you're speaking, though, you should be firmly rooted into the ground for most of the time. Think of yourself as a tree where the bottom half of your body is the trunk and fixed and the top half is the branches which can move in the breeze. Some people do a little nervous dance on the spot, it's called the 'speaker samba', but you should avoid it. Definitely don't pace up and down in front of the audience, that's called the 'trainer's trek' and will completely distract them. Another fidget is to check the time by looking at your watch. If you've rehearsed your presentation, you will know how long it takes. And finally please try not to wring your hands or rub the back of your neck as they're classic signs of anxiety.

- **FILLERS.** Fillers are very difficult to suppress. They are the little noises we make and the words we say when we're thinking about what to say next. Noises like, "Umm, hah, mmmm" and words like "Okay, well, next, so." Some people have their own pet phrase, which can quickly get on the audience's nerves. Things like, "Basically, fundamentally, I think." The only way to eliminate these is to discover which ones you do. That means that you must listen to your presentation when you rehearsed it into your tape recorder. Check for fillers and try and eliminate them next time. Remember you're not on the radio so you don't need to worry about a second or two of silence. When you're thinking about what to say next, shut your mouth and say nothing.

THE POWER STANCE

When you first get up onto that stage (real or proverbial) to present, you need to radiate confidence and feel the power in yourself. You need to adopt what's called the 'power stance'. Think about what happens when two dogs meet. They both adopt a posture to establish which is the most dominant animal. They raise themselves up to their full height, lift their heads and stiffen their ears so they are erect. They create presence and you need to do the same when you speak.

1. Men, if you've got a single-breasted jacket, undo it. Otherwise you'll look like a stuffed chicken. Take your hands out of your pockets.

2. Stand in the middle of the room directly in front of the audience with your legs hip width apart. Both your legs should be straight with soft knees and not locked.

3. Roll your shoulders back so you raise your arms and open your chest. Lift your hands so they are at waist height. Either keep them apart or place the back of one hand into the palm of the other.

4. Clench your toes and move the weight onto the balls of your feet. This is why it's called 'on your toes'.

5. Arch your neck back and raise your head and then drop your chin so you're looking down at the audience from underneath your eyelids. It's called the Diana or Elvis look.

BODY LANGUAGE *doesn't have to be all about tight control and restricting movement. In a zippy, passionate pitch for KCO Iceblading in Series 7, Karen Coombes leapt up and span in the air to demonstrate the kind of move possible with their special kind of inline skates. If it's relevant to the pitch and doesn't obfuscate what the business is about, a bit of dynamism can inject life into a presentation and keep an audience's attention.*

The power stance will feel uncomfortable and unnatural when you first try and do it, but why not try it now? Just remember…

HIP WIDTH
SHOULDERS BACK
ON YOUR TOES
HEAD UP
CHIN DOWN

THE RELAXED STANCE

We looked at this in Commandment 6 (see p130). It's the stance that you adopt during the Q&A session, and also when informally chatting with the audience before and after you do your presentation. (It's where you have one leg straight and one bent slightly at the knee. Your foot turned out so your hip doesn't tilt and all your weight on your straight leg.)

When you first try the relaxed stance yourself you'll find it awkward and maybe a bit uncomfortable. But persevere and you'll soon look (and feel) calm and confident. It's the stance that you should always use when you're chatting to a stranger, either at a networking event or a party.

The relaxed and power stance are neutral, and you should look grounded. If you stand with your feet too close together, you look as if you could easily be pushed over, and people will subliminally think you are literally a pushover, easy prey. And if you stand with your feet too far apart they'll see you as argumentative and threatening. The relaxed stance is neutral. You're not a pushover and you're not looking for trouble either.

LET THEM FEEL YOUR PASSION

Earlier we talked about the body as a tree with your legs firmly rooted into the ground and your upper half swaying in the breeze. If you are doing this, then you can freely use gestures with your arms, hands and face to show your passion, and your eyes to engage with the audience on a personal level.

- **MAKE OPEN GESTURES.** Use your arms and hands to make gestures that are appropriate to what you're talking about. You must not look like you're conducting an orchestra, but when you talk about the future you can make a big open gesture with both your arms up. Gestures must be open, in other words with your elbows away from your body. The bigger the audience, the bigger the gesture. You use your fingers to count points like first, second and third. It helps the audience understand whereabouts you are. But never point at the audience because it's an aggressive posture. However, the worst possible thing would be if you were to stand rigid and barely move at all – if you're passionate about something then you must show it.

- **ANIMATE YOUR FACE AND HEAD.** You don't want to look rigid, so move and tilt your head to look around the room, and let your passion show through your facial expressions during your presentation. During your question and answer session, however, you need to be much more guarded with your facial expressions. Adopt the neutral mask and steady gaze described on pp132–3 whilst someone is asking you a question, so that you don't give away any emotional response (e.g. irritation, worry) to the question being asked. Especially keep your eyebrows under control.

- **WATCH THE AUDIENCE.** You have to engage with every person in the audience so they feel that you're talking to them and thus can feel your passion personally. You can't look at them all at once but you should try to look at every single person for a couple of seconds in turn. Make sure that you move your head, not just your eyes, to look at them, because you want it to be obvious that you're looking at them and also you don't want your eyes to seem shifty. If you look closely at the audience in this way you will also get feedback and see if they are picking up and responding to the passion you are showing or, conversely, looking bored.

SO MUCH TO LEARN

The challenge with body language is that there is so much to remember, both with interpreting the audience's body language and controlling your own. The main thing to do, though, is eliminate the worst of your bad habits and mannerisms. So either video one of your rehearsals or ask a friend to watch you, then mark off your points on this checklist.

GOOD POINTS

- Stance should be relaxed, rooted and upright.
- Looking at ALL the audience.
- Wide and appropriate gestures.
- Animated facial expressions and tilting head during presentation; neutral during questioning.
- Variable voice – pitch, pace, pause and inflections.

BAD POINTS

- Fidgeting with pens, pointers, etc.
- Wringing or clenched hands, picking at fingernails.
- Playing with jewellery, hair, etc.
- Pacing up and down, shifting weight or dancing on the spot.
- Arms folded or hands akimbo on hips.
- Pointing with fingers or fist.
- Frowning, darting or squinting eyes.

CASE STUDY **FROM SERIES 7 EPISODE 8**

MOTORMOUSE

David and Patti Bailey's business had been running for only about five months when they visited the Den. Their business centred on high-quality wireless computer mice styled as classic sports cars. The couple were experienced in business, and the pitch was assured and engaging, their body language expressing confidence and openness.

THE BAILEYS *cut a dash in the Den, looking sophisticated and in control throughout.*

Because their product was small, the Baileys needed to think carefully about how best to showcase the motormouse. They also needed for it to be taken seriously, so they needed to look serious too. To accomplish this, they dressed in dark clothing, with just a splash of colour from David's red tie. They looked sophisticated, well-matched in appearance, and their dark clothes acted as a backdrop to the bright but small computer mouse.

Because of the constraints of filming on set, the entrepreneurs have to stand in a certain spot. However, stance, hand positions, head posture, movement and facial expressions all tell a story. Patti held her hands together, but they were not overly clasped – just enough to stop any distracting movements. David used his hands very deliberately, almost like a magician, to point out the finer details of the product, whilst, in their speech, the pitch moved seamlessly between the two. They both smiled easily and naturally, and looked directly at the person they were speaking to.

THE MOTORMOUSE *is superbly detailed and produced to a high standard.*

Though the Baileys clearly won over their audience, four of the Dragons felt the potential market was too small to be worth investment. James was looking beyond the one product, though, and saw an opportunity. He offered them a deal in which he'd give them more than the investment they'd asked for (£120,000 rather than £100,000) and in return would use the Baileys' skills for presentation and consultancy for his own businesses. It was a good bit of negotiation that seemed to result in a pretty equitable outcome.

FOLLOWING THE DEAL STRUCK IN THE DEN, *the Baileys now investigate companies that apply to James in order to gauge their prospects. David himself invests in them through Bailey Development Ltd, of which James Caan is now a shareholder.*

COMMANDMENT 9

PREPARE MENTALLY

Can you train your brain to overcome those nerves?

THE THOUGHT OF HAVING TO GIVE A PITCH on which your future may depend is sobering, to say the least. Many surveys have been done into the things that scare us most, and public speaking usually tops the list, ahead of bugs and spiders, and even the fear of death! But nerves needn't be paralysing. There are lots of things you can do to prepare yourself mentally for the 'ordeal'. Some techniques take time and you'll need to practise them in the few weeks before your pitch. Others you can do on the day, and we'll include those in Commandment 10. The techniques tune your brain away from negative thoughts to a positive state.

IMAGINE YOUR DREAM

One of the best ways to overcome your fear of pitching is to think in terms of your dream.

1. Imagine what will happen if you are successful, how it will change your life.

2. Write what it would mean in 20 words or fewer. For example, victory at achieving the deal; opening up of wonderful opportunities; ability to afford a fantastic car.

3. Now translate your words into mental images, sounds and feelings. For instance, you might vividly see a Ferrari in your drive, hear the sound of a private plane, or feel the real excitement of getting the deal.

4. So rather than simply using the word 'success', you should be experiencing what you'll see, hear and feel when you achieve success.

5. When you've thought of your image, find a physical picture or photograph that conjures up your dream in your mind. This will help you channel any negative thoughts into positive energy. Some of the most successful salespeople have a picture of their dream car stuck on the mirror in their bathroom. Every morning before they start work they see and remember their dream – it's what they are working for.

This technique of visualizing success is part of Neuro Linguistic Programming (NLP), which is used in business coaching. Some people talk about what they want – the outcome – rather than their dream. But 'dream' is probably a better word here as 'outcome' can be confused with goals and objectives. They're not the same. A goal or objective is just a step on the way to achieving your dream. It can be something like "To stop smoking", which is a negative thing. Or "To be promoted to the next management level", which is positive.

Goals and objectives are expressed in words. Dreams are expressed as images and feelings. And they're all about using your imagination to motivate, inspire you and make things happen.

When you're passionate about your dream, your focus is external. When you're emotional, your focus is your own ego – the fear of failure. But if you want something really badly enough (your dream), you will focus on achieving it, and work out how you can overcome each of your negative feelings and turn them into positive actions.

" YOU ARE WHAT YOU THINK, NOT WHAT YOU THINK YOU ARE "

NEW THOUGHT MOVEMENT

THE LAW OF ATTRACTION

This 'law' first gained popularity in the early 1900s as part of the New Thought Movement. The principles are encapsulated by the phrase, "You are what you think, not what you think you are." It builds on the Hindu view that if we focus on something, God will make it happen. In 1937 Napoleon Hill wrote a book called *Think and Grow Rich*, in which each chapter contained a secret on how your thoughts can make you achieve success. A DVD called *The Secret* appeared on the internet in 2006 and gained world-wide attention through viral marketing, which is where people tell their friends about something.

Today many people recognize that The Law of Attraction is a proven phenomenon which has three steps.

- **ASK** – Have a clear idea of what you want and visualize it as something tangible. The image that is your dream.

- **BELIEVE** – Focus your thoughts on your dream and believe that it will happen. The photograph on your bathroom mirror will help you with this.

- **RECEIVE** – Notice what's happening and be open to opportunities.

The key point with The Law of Attraction is that you have to believe in yourself and banish any negative thoughts. Then it will happen.

BELIEVE IN YOURSELF

What makes us form notions about ourselves that may not be true? Things such as not liking a particular type of food or drink even though we've never tasted it. We've all heard people say something like, "I know I just wouldn't like it." We all sometimes get similar

A BIG PART OF PREPARATION FOR THE DEN *involves anticipating the kinds of questions that the Dragons will ask. Some of these are easy to guess and are directly related to the kind of business proposition being offered, its finances and the market potential. But they like to dig deeper, on occasions, to find out about the background of the people pitching. Rachel Watkyn (left) of the Tiny Box Company appeared in Series 6 and, as she later admitted, was totally unprepared for this level of scrutiny. "Theo asking these questions was really quite difficult, because I'd had a lot to contend with in the previous years and I just wasn't mentally prepared for it at all." Despite feeling this, she told the Dragons about how she'd contracted a life-threatening illness after going into hospital for a routine operation, and how this had led to her losing her job and house. Entrepreneurship is often a transformative activity, and Rachel's opening up about her past made her, in the words of Peter Jones, "very investable".*

negative notions about ourselves and our abilities. We say things along the lines of, "I would never do that, I just couldn't do it." Or, "I'd be no good at that." And when we say it we convince ourselves that we can't do it, so our prophecy becomes true.

It's the same for a golfer who's just about to strike their ball when someone says, "Watch that bunker on your right." Now rather than ignoring it, their focus switches to the bunker instead of the pin. It's almost as though the bunker attracts the ball so it lands in the sand, not on the green.

You must learn how to banish any negative thoughts that you might have. The problem is that our brains like to dwell on the fear of failure. But if you focus on your dream, you will clear the mess in your head. When you've got to do the frightening thing called the pitch, concentrate on your dream. If you believe in yourself you will turn your negative emotions of fear into a positive passion for what you want.

TRICK YOUR BRAIN WITH AN ANCHOR

Some people carry a trinket or wear a piece of clothing for luck. In reality, luck doesn't play much of a part in success, but the lucky charm can trick the brain into feeling good, so we do something well.

In Neuro Linguistic Programming it's called anchoring. It actually comes from Classical Conditioning, which was researched in the late 19th century. Ivan Pavlov was one of its pioneers when in the 1890s he discovered that dogs can be conditioned into expecting food by the sound of a metronome or bell.

Then in 1920 John Watson, one of the founders of behaviourism, conducted an experiment with a child called Albert that demonstrated that humans could also be tricked into a particular mental state by an external trigger. In Albert's case the trigger was the sight of a white furry object such as a rabbit and even the beard of Santa Claus.

Classical conditioning can happen to us all at any time. For example if you've ever had a bad fall from a horse at some time in your life or a nasty car accident, every time you see a horse or a similar car to the one in your accident your mind will recall how it felt at the time – not pleasant.

If you want to exploit this phenomenon of anchoring, you will have to create a trigger that tricks your mind into reliving a previous experience. On your pitch you need to be calm and confident so you must condition yourself to relive a previous time when you were calm, confident and successful.

1. Stand up and think about the last time you felt that way.

2. Relive the moment and circumstances in your head. Then imagine how you felt at the time and visualize the scene around you.

3. Now you need to create your trigger that will anchor it in your head. It's a bit like Pavlov's dogs who were conditioned by a bell to expect food. Your trigger could be noise, the sight of an object or a feeling. For instance you say "Powerful" under your breath whilst you clench your toes or press your thumb into the tip of your forefinger.

4. When you've chosen your trigger you will need to condition yourself to respond to it by practising it quite a few times. Get yourself into the calm and confident state and then apply your trigger.

5. Eventually your trigger alone will stimulate the calm and confident state – that's when you know you have an anchor.

NEIL AND LAURA WESTWOOD *presented the Magic Whiteboard to the Dragons in Series 6. Their level of preparation showed not only in their confident and enthusiastic pitch but also in their targeting of a particular Dragon. So while Duncan made them an offer and Deborah matched it (they had noted her interest by a twitch of her fingers), Neil and Laura zoned in on Theo, the Dragon they wanted most to fast-track the national distribution of their products. The pitch was geared towards getting Theo on board, and it worked. He made them an offer, the final deal being a joint investment from Theo and Deborah.*

Anchoring, or Classical Conditioning, techniques are also used by advertisers and film makers. Think about the film *Jaws*. Every time the shark appeared the audience was conditioned by the music. After a couple of times it only took a few bars of that music to make the audience's hands sweat and hearts beat faster. The particular crescendo of music was the trigger.

EXERCISE YOUR MIND

Professional speakers train their brain to think quickly. What they practise is impromptu speaking for a couple of minutes on a random subject. You can do the same when alone or with a colleague.

" THE MIND IS ITS OWN PLACE AND CAN MAKE A HEAVEN OF HELL "

JOHN MILTON (1608–74), ENGLISH POET

1. Take a dozen of your business cards and on the back of each write the name of a famous building or place such as the Tower of London, Houses of Parliament, Edinburgh and so on. Make some of them easy, like Disneyland and Las Vegas, and make some of them harder, like Milton Keynes and Doncaster.

2. Find a kitchen timer or stopwatch and set it for two minutes. Then shuffle the cards and place them written-side down on a table.

3. Stand up and imagine an audience, pick a card and look what you've written on it. Put it down, start the timer and speak for two minutes on the subject.

The more you do it, the quicker your brain will think. The key thing is not to think too hard about the words, just open your mouth and say the first thing that comes into your head. To make it easier you might like to say the words on the card as the first sentence. So you could say, "Milton Keynes reminds me of the time that..." Practise a few times during the days before your pitch and you'll be surprised how quickly you can think when you are under pressure.

THE POWER OF YOUR BREATH

In Commandment 7 we talked about the power of your voice and looked at how breathing can help you improve your voice control. Focusing on your breath is also a very powerful way of calming yourself down, relaxing you and making you feel good about yourself. In other words, switching you into a positive frame of mind.

You should always try and take some time out a couple of times a day to have a 'calm breathing' break. It takes only two or three minutes, but it will help focus your mind, retune you to a positive attitude and boost your self belief.

1 Sit in an upright chair somewhere quiet where you won't be disturbed. Make sure that you're upright and place the palms of your hands on top of your thighs, just like those statues that show how the ancient Egyptians used to sit. You'll need to look straight ahead and then close your eyes.

2 You're now going to take six low, deep breaths through your nose and down into your stomach. You need to take

" MAINTAINING A STATE OF INNER CALM WILL HELP YOU TO KEEP A COOL HEAD WHEN OTHERS BECOME HEATED AND ANGRY "

DADI JANKI, BRAHMA KUMARIS SPIRITUAL UNIVERSITY

them slowly so that each complete in and out breath takes about 15 seconds. In other words, about four a minute. With each breath you say the following words to yourself, one on the in breath and the other as you slowly exhale.

FIRST BREATH "IN, OUT"
SECOND "DEEP, SLOW"
THIRD "CALM, EASY"
FOURTH "SMILE, RELEASE"
FIFTH "PRESENT, MOMENT"
SIXTH "WONDERFUL, DREAM"

3 When you've finished this take a final slow breath and then slowly open your eyes. Sit for a few seconds and then go back to what you were doing before.

What you've just done is a short, two-minute meditation where you focused on your breath. It's a technique used in Raja yoga and it's a wonderful way to recharge your brain and make you feel calm again.

RELEASE YOUR ENDORPHINS WITH A POWER MOVE

Every professional speaker has what's called a 'power move', which releases any tension in their shoulders and warms up their voice. They also use it to produce endorphins. These are the feel-good hormones and are sometimes called the runner's high. They give you a feeling of power and control over yourself.

Ideally, try to do a power move less than half an hour before your pitch (see p211). It's worth practising in the days before the big event. This simple 'power move' has four easy yoga movements.

1. **SHRUG.** Raise your shoulders towards your ears as high as you can with your arms down by your sides. Hold for about three seconds.

2. **HUG.** Imagine you're giving a bear-hug to a large person. Put your arms around them and hold it for two or three seconds.

3. **SQUEEZE.** Hold your hands together behind your back and raise them up with your arms outstretched so you squeeze your shoulder-blades together. Hold this for a couple of seconds.

4. **STRETCH.** Raise your arms above your head and reach for the stars. Release after three seconds and relax.

When you have done that you should warm up your voice by doing your mouth exercises and your tongue twisters (see p153).

" TELL THEM WHAT YOU'RE GOING TO TELL THEM, TELL THEM IT AND THEN TELL THEM WHAT YOU'VE TOLD THEM " ANON

SHARON WRIGHT OF MAGNAMOLE *(see pp34–5) gave this insight into pitching in the Den. "Confidence is power: don't be afraid to challenge what they [the Dragons] say – in a diplomatic way and without arrogance. After all, no one knows your product like you do."*

PRACTISE YOUR OPENING AND CLOSE

Research has shown that the parts of your speech people will remember most are your opening, your close and anything else you repeat two or three times. For this reason you should say what you're about to tell them at the start of your presentation and summarize it again at the end. The repetition is what they remember.

- Your opening line grabs the audience's attention but it's your closing line that they take away in their heads.

- Many professional speakers will write their closing sentence before they even think about the words in the rest of their presentation. Because the opening and closing are so important, you must actually write them down and rehearse them. They're not long, probably about 20 or 50 words each, but they are very important.

PATTI AND DAVID BAILEY *(see pp186–7) seemed very relaxed in the Den. But David reveals that the 'natural and controlled' approach was a result of extensive research, rehearsals and pre-learned data. "We studied DVDs for weeks and practised angles of eye contact and responses. Whilst you can never be totally sure of who is going to ask what, we were fairly sure and therefore prepared accordingly."*

- On the day itself you should put your opening line in your pocket. Then just before you meet your audience you can take one final glance at it. So even though you'll be nervous when you start, you know exactly what your first few words are going to be.

- Finally, if you suffer very badly from nerves you should also get some Bach's Rescue Remedy, stocked by most pharmacies. It is a traditional herbal remedy for nerves. You can get it in the form of drops or as a mouth spray and it will help you relax, get focused and stay calm.

GIVE YOURSELF TIME TO CONQUER YOUR FEARS

The thing about mental preparation is that it takes time. Like building up the content of your pitch, you can't mentally prepare from scratch the day before and expect to be on top form. All athletes and sports people train hard and get themselves psyched up over many days in the build-up to their big event which may itself last only a few minutes. Learn from athletes and mentally work up to your pitch as though you've entered for a marathon.

You must think of your dream as soon as you can and start to practise anchoring. Take some time out every lunchtime to do your 'power move' and your voice exercises. If you work on your quick thinking once or twice a week, you'll be surprised how much faster and sharper your mind will become generally.

Make the mental exercises in this chapter routine so they become second nature and part of your working life. Then, when the day of your pitch arrives you'll be ready for anything they can throw at you. And remember, the skills you will have learnt will not be wasted, no matter what the outcome of the pitch is.

Commandment 10 covers the order of doing things on the day itself, including ways to relax yourself at various points.

" I BELIEVE THAT ANYONE CAN CONQUER FEAR BY DOING THE THINGS HE FEARS TO DO "

ELEANOR ROOSEVELT (1884–1962), US FIRST LADY

CASE STUDY **FROM SERIES 7 EPISODE 6**

TECH 21

Jason Roberts kept his composure and remained a calm figure in a Den that grew to a simmer as the Dragons scrutinized his business and tore into his valuation of the company he owned, Tech 21.

The business was in the manufacture and retail of protective carrying cases for mobile phones and laptops, its USP being the use of a revolutionary material called d3o – pliable in its normal state, instantly rigid on impact.

The presentation began in a measured way, with Jason introducing the products. Theo then began a line of questioning about Jason's background to tee up his real question: why was Jason offering only 5% of his business for £150,000?

TECH 21'S *protective slip cases for the iPhone.*

Jason countered with some impressive trading figures for the current year, but then Peter ratcheted up the pressure: "What is your reasoning for valuing this at £3 million?" Maintaining his calm disposition, Jason outlined contracts he had for substantial orders. This wasn't enough to persuade James, who embarked on a quick round of questioning about the current finances of

Tech 21. Jason struggled to think of figures and by the time he had regained his composure, James has declared himself out. Duncan followed suit, citing the £3 million valuation as an overestimate.

This was a low point for Jason, but he stayed confident and composed. He revealed a further deal for an ongoing supply of laptop cases with an American firm. Theo, Deborah and Peter were all interested now. Jason's company clearly had potential for growth. The valuation was still an issue, though, and Jason ultimately had to decide whether he could accept a deal with Peter and Theo in exchange for 40% equity. Reasoning that Theo and Peter would add great value to the business and that, by taking a large stake, they would have a greater incentive to make the company successful, Jason took the deal.

JASON DEMONSTRATED *the tensile qualities of d3o, then faced a thorough question and answer session, absorbing the questions and replying in measured terms, before concluding a deal with Peter and Theo.*

COMMANDMENT 10

SEIZE THE DAY

Are you ready?

YOUR BIG DAY HAS FINALLY ARRIVED and all you have to do now is seize the opportunity. But you're ready. You've rehearsed your presentation, gone through the questions you think they'll ask and prepared both your mind and body for what's ahead. Here we'll assume that you're giving the pitch to people you've not dealt with before, and at a venue you've not been to before. We'll walk you through each step of the day, with checklists and reminders about what you're doing when. We'll show you how to cope with any last-minute hiccups and also how to draw your pitch to a natural close and come out feeling positive, whatever the outcome.

Good luck!

GET ALL YOUR STUFF TOGETHER

Gather everything you need the night before, then check it again in the morning for your own peace of mind. Here's a checklist.

- **THE OUTFIT** you'll be wearing that will project a positive, professional image of yourself.
- **PROPS AND PRODUCT SAMPLES** in a box or bag.
- **YOUR VISUALS AND COPIES OF THE TAKE-AWAY PACK** in your briefcase or bag.
- **THE NOTES FOR YOUR STRUCTURE** in your pocket. They will be your comfort blanket in the unlikely event you freeze.
- **A COPY OF YOUR OPENING LINES** written out in full. Put them in another pocket, you don't want to mix them up with your notes.
- **BACH'S RESCUE REMEDY**, either the mouth spray or some drops put in a bottle of water.
- **A COPY OF TODAY'S NEWSPAPER** or a magazine so you have something to take your mind off your pitch while you wait in reception.
- **DIRECTIONS TO THE VENUE AND CONTACT NAMES.** Try to memorize the contact names, but write them down as a reminder.

" SUCCESS DEPENDS ON RECOGNIZING WHEN YOUR MOMENT HAS COME "

DUNCAN BANNATYNE, DRAGON

CASE STUDY **FROM SERIES 4 EPISODE 1**

IGLOO

Anthony Coates-Smith and Alistair Turner pitched for a business that couriered chilled deliveries. Duncan Bannatyne made the first offer: half the money for 20%. Rather than waiting to get a matching offer from another Dragon, Alistair politely recountered that they could achieve the investment at a lower cost to them by going to the bank for a loan rather than giving up 40% equity.

The Dragons accepted this rationale, and former Dragon Richard Farleigh suggested that he and Duncan join forces for a 15% stake each. "That's still 30% of a successful, growing business," Alistair reminded them. Deborah and Theo then matched offers for a combined 25% stake, and Peter offered the entire sum for 30% or half for 12.5%.

ANTHONY AND ALISTAIR'S IGLOO BUSINESS *made a loss in the first year, then grew in years two and three to make a decent profit.*

With all five Dragons offering, the duo had leverage. They turned back to Duncan and Richard to ask if they would improve their offer, and the pair came in with a joint stake of 22.5%. Throughout, Alistair and Anthony were careful with their words and arguments. Now it was time to seize the moment, and they took Duncan and Richard's offer.

READY YOUR MIND AND BODY

- **HAVE A LIGHT MEAL A COUPLE OF HOURS BEFORE YOU LEAVE.** Nothing spicy, no coffee, no tea and definitely no alcohol. The coffee and tea will dull your voice and the alcohol will dull your brain. And you don't want indigestion.

- **LISTEN TO YOUR FAVOURITE PIECE OF MUSIC ON THE WAY THERE.** This will get you in a good mood. Do not listen to the news as it will just depress you.

- **TIME YOUR JOURNEY TO ALLOW FOR POSSIBLE DELAYS IN GETTING TO THE VENUE.** That will probably mean getting to the vicinity with more than 15 minutes to spare, so you can wait somewhere nearby until it's nearer the time to go in. Turn your mobile to silent now, so you don't have to remember to do it once you're at the venue.

- **GO TO THE VENUE SLIGHTLY BEFORE YOU'RE DUE.** It's best to time your actual arrival to be five to ten minutes early so you can spend a few moments getting yourself in the mood. Prepare yourself mentally to be taking in new names and faces within a few minutes.

ENTER THE VENUE (... 'THE DEN')

- **START PERFORMING AS SOON AS YOU REACH THE VENUE.** You never know who's looking out of the window.

- **TREAT THE RECEPTIONIST IN A FRIENDLY, COURTEOUS AND PROFESSIONAL WAY.** Politely decline coffee or tea as you don't want to fill your bladder. It's also difficult to juggle a coffee cup with your briefcase and your box of props when someone comes to collect you.

- **FIND THE LOOS.** If you're kept waiting in reception for more than a few moments, it's a good idea to find the toilet at this point and do the 'power move' (see p200) to release any tension from the journey, unleash your endorphins and warm up your voice.

"THIS IS THE PRECEPT BY WHICH I HAVE LIVED: PREPARE FOR THE WORST; EXPECT THE BEST; AND TAKE WHAT COMES"

ROBERT E. SPEER, AMERICAN PREACHER

- **KEEP YOURSELF CALM.** When you get back to the reception area sit down and rehearse your opening. When you've done that get your newspaper from your briefcase and calmly read it. You can just leave it in reception when they come to collect you. If you start to get anxious do a 'calm breathing' break with your eyes open in case the receptionist sees you do it. Or take a shot of your rescue remedy.

- **STAND UP WHEN SOMEONE COMES TO COLLECT YOU.** Say, "hello" and shake hands. Always be friendly and look relaxed – you may not know who this person actually is yet, or what power they have.

- **POSSIBLE EQUIPMENT SET-UP STAGE.** Depending on the circumstances, it may be that you have been given the opportunity to arrive early to set up your equipment before the actual pitch is due to take place. In this case, you will probably be taken to an empty room and will have a specified amount of time in which to prepare, for example, PowerPoint or other audio-visual equipment, whiteboard and props. If you haven't been offered this stage, then you will be taken to a room with your audience already in it, and you should act as follows.

MAKE AN ENTRANCE

- **CHECK THE SITUATION.** When you're about to meet the audience, take a low deep breath and stand tall. Remember what we said in Commandment 8 about one step at a time and not rushing. If you've just got to the room with your audience in it, don't walk in yet, just take two steps and put your briefcase and box of props down just inside the door. Then look around the room and see what's happening. They might be standing around chatting, or they might be sat around a table waiting for you.

CASE STUDY **FROM SERIES 4 EPISODE 1**

KUCCI KUKUI

With a background working in pharmaceuticals, Dr Gili Kucci asked the Dragons for £100,000 for investment in Kucci Kukui massage therapies and products. Gili made a confident presentation, explaining the USP of her skin-care products – that they used Hawaiian kukui oil, which was good for skin conditions such as eczema and rich in vitamins and antioxidants. She also clearly articulated how she would spend the investment to expand the business and increase its product range.

GILI LATER SAID OF THE DRAGONS:
"I've got nothing against them, because I got my figures wrong."

However, the pitch fell through a hole when the Dragons began to quiz Gili over the past and present finances of the business. Gili mistook questions about turnover for questions about profit and conflated real numbers from the past with projected figures for the current year. She didn't get any offers from the Dragons.

Outside the Den, Gili was offered £163,000 investment for 24% of her company by another backer. She also enlisted model Sophie Anderton for marketing the company's skin care products. However, the Kucci Kukui company later foundered and went into liquidation in 2009.

THE FIRST FEW MINUTES

- **IDENTIFY YOUR PRIME CONTACT.** If the audience is sitting, your prime contact will probably stand up to greet you. On the other hand if people are milling around chatting, walk slowly into the room to greet whoever comes to meet you. Shake hands in a friendly and confident manner. This person will hopefully then probably introduce you to everyone else in the room.

- **IDENTIFY AND ACKNOWLEDGE THE OTHERS.** You will have done your homework and know at least some of the names of the people in the audience, and what those people do. If possible try and shake hands with everybody, although this might be difficult if there's a table in the way, or there are very many people. If you can't shake hands, then at least acknowledge each of them as they're introduced and say hello with a warm smile. Memorize the names if you can.

- **TRY TO GAUGE PEOPLE'S FEELINGS AND MOOD.** There might be quite a few minutes of polite small talk and chatter before you actually get started. Look at the eyes of everyone you chat with and be friendly, but stay clear of business or your idea at this time. Just mention the weather, your journey, their premises or the view from the window. Although you haven't yet started your pitch you will already be making an impression on them.

- **USE THE 'CROSS-EYE' GAZE.** You might be in close proximity to people at this stage, and you must make sure you don't appear to stare. So it's probably best to use the 'cross-eye' gaze. This means that you look diagonally across at one eye and then switch to the other. So with your right eye you look at their right eye and then with your left eye you look at their left eye. It's a gaze, not a stare, and respectful, not rude. What's more the other person won't realize that you're looking with one eye. You'll find it easier to hold eye contact with them over a long period of time, but it does take practice.

- **TRY AND DETERMINE WHO IS THE DECISION MAKER.** If the group is sitting around a table, the decision maker will usually be sat in the power position with their back to the window and furthest from the door. Give this person a friendly smile with a firm handshake and don't allow yourself to feel intimidated.

- **IF STANDING, ADOPT YOUR RELAXED STANCE.** Stand in the relaxed stance that we talked about in Commandment 8 – one leg straight, one leg bent.

- **IF YOU ARE OFFERED A SEAT, PLACE YOURSELF RIGHT BACK IN THE CHAIR.** If you sit on the edge of the seat, you'll look tense and anxious. If you lounge back, you'll look too relaxed. Sit upright and try not to shuffle around in the seat as this will fuel your nerves. When you talk,

EDDIE MIDDLETON MADE A PITCH FOR HIS PATIO HEATERS (NOW BRANDED AS CHILLCHASERS) *in Series 7. The electric heaters produce less carbon than gas heaters and so have some ecological credentials. The products appealed to some of the Dragons, in particular James and Peter, who had seen this market starting to take off in the US. But Eddie blew the pitch when it came to the Dragons' exploration of his business plan. Initially Eddie was resistant to giving the Dragons the figures they asked for in relation to the costs of production, wholesale and retail, explaining that it was sensitive information. This antagonized the Dragons and put Eddie in a weak bargaining position because of it. So, while Peter and James were still interested enough in the products to make an offer, they were pretty inflexible in regard to the amount of equity they wanted (48%), citing Eddie's attitude as one of the reasons for this. Eddie had sensibly set a limit in his mind on how much equity he was prepared to release (35%) and so negotiations then ended without a deal.*

"A PESSIMIST SEES THE DIFFICULTY IN EVERY OPPORTUNITY; AN OPTIMIST SEES THE OPPORTUNITY IN EVERY DIFFICULTY" WINSTON CHURCHILL

lean slightly forward in your seat and use your arms to make appropriate gestures. When you're listening, place your hands calmly on your lap.

- **START SETTING UP YOUR THINGS.** When the introductions and small talk are over fetch your bags from by the door and calmly set up all the things for your pitch. Take your time and respond confidently if they chat to you whilst you're doing this.

WHAT TO DO IF SOMETHING GOES WRONG

Of course, there are always some things outside your control, and probably numerous things that can go wrong before you even start your pitch. The following scenarios are all quite common for people trying to give a presentation.

- **THE VENUE IS CHANGED AT SHORT NOTICE.** Sometimes they can move the venue at the last minute and you end up in a rush. Don't panic, it's not your fault, so just take your time and get there when you can. If you get held up for a long time, then call – it's what mobile phones are for.

CASE STUDY **FROM SERIES 7 EPISODE 1**

TRUECALL

Steve Smith gave an assured pitch for his trueCall nuisance call blocking device, and forecast profits rising rapidly from a modest £15,000 in 2009 to £1.5 million in 2012.

Despite Steve's confident presentation, Duncan expressed reservations about the unit price and Peter suggested that it ought to have been incorporated into a telephone handset rather than be sold as a separate product. These were robust arguments.

But Steve's confidence was underpinned by a strong business pedigree. He had been successful before, and, when he revealed that he had already invested £700,000 in trueCall, using some of the £6.5 million he had accrued from the sale of two previous businesses, all the Dragons' ears pricked up.

STEVE DEMONSTRATED *the product in action, whilst explaining the problem it solved; then he articulated some impressive business projections and future profits.*

With Steve's business credibility riding high in the Den, the bidding began. James was first to make an offer: £50,000 for 12.5%. Deborah countered with the full £100,000 for 12.5%, just 2.5% more equity than Steve initially offered. Duncan offered to match whatever Peter decided to offer. Peter then reminded Steve of the value of his own telecoms credentials before offering the full amount for 15%; he was also happy to share the investment, however, with Duncan and James.

Not to be outdone, Theo reminded Steve that he can provide instant UK-wide distribution. He matched Deborah's offer and, in response, Deborah offered a joint deal with Theo. Steve now had to assess this situation quickly and consider not just what was on the table, but what deal would be best for him. He expressed his worries about splitting the equity between two or more Dragons because of how this might adversely affect their level of input. Seizing the moment, he homed in on Peter, asking if he would agree to put in the full investment for 10%. Peter countered with 12.5%, and this they agreed upon. It was an exciting and worthwhile piece of brinkmanship.

STEVE GAVE CAREFUL THOUGHT *to the various offers he had received – single offers from Deborah and Peter, as well as joint offers from James, Duncan and Peter, and separately from Theo and Deborah. All were good offers, but Steve wanted the attention of a single investor. He approached Peter with a final piece of negotiation for a great outcome.*

- **YOU ARE KEPT WAITING IN RECEPTION FOR AGES.** This is a distinct possibility and can really upset some people. Do not have a coffee while you wait as this will dehydrate you and make you want to go to the toilet. Sit quietly and do the two-minute 'calm breathing' break that we talked about in the previous chapter. Then read a newspaper or magazine. And wait. Try not to look at your watch as it will irritate you more. Instead just try and stay calm.

- **YOU REALIZE THAT THE DECISION MAKER IS MISSING.** At the last minute the key person in the audience drops out. This is disheartening but there's nothing you can actually do about it. Go through your pitch as planned and leave the extra take-away pack for the decision maker. The following day phone them to check that they received it and try to arrange a one-to-one meeting to talk it through with them.

- **THE TECHNOLOGY DOESN'T WORK FOR YOU.** This can be one of the challenges with PowerPoint. If you can't get it working in the first place, then ask your key contact to delay the beginning of your presentation for about 15 minutes. Try not to fiddle in front of the audience as you'll get very flustered. If the technology breaks halfway through, then suggest a recess for about a quarter of an hour. If you can't fix the problem in 15 minutes, ask if a flip chart or whiteboard is available. If yes, then position it near you and start your presentation. You can write the key points and figures on the flip chart or whiteboard as you go. If there's not even a flip chart available, remember that you have copies of all your visuals in your take-away pack. Make a light-hearted joke and don't panic: the audience will understand.

> **" OH THE NERVES, THE NERVES; THE MYSTERIES OF THIS MACHINE CALLED MAN! OH THE LITTLE THAT UNHINGES IT, POOR CREATURES THAT WE ARE! "**
>
> CHARLES DICKENS

ZERO HOUR

- **TAKE POSITION.** If you're seated, stand up to begin your pitch. Although you may already have mixed with the audience, your nerves might overwhelm you when you stand up. If this happens, step a bit closer to them so it almost becomes intimate. Imagine they're just your friends.

- **TAKE A LOW BREATH AND GET INTO YOUR POWER STANCE.** Grasp the nettle with both hands and calmly say, "Ladies and gentlemen, good morning." Then pause to allow them to reply. (It's interesting to note that if you say, "Good morning, ladies and gentlemen," they are less likely to say anything in response.)

- **THANK YOUR AUDIENCE FOR COMING.** Say something like, "First I'd like to thank you all for sparing me the time to see you today."

- **THEN PAUSE AND DELIVER YOUR OPENING LINE.** Now you've started your pitch and you must listen to your own voice for 20 minutes. You're going to be nervous so you will start to speak too fast and you'll need to make a conscious effort to slow it. This will calm you and help you concentrate on using your normal voice and clearly pronouncing the words.

- **REMEMBER YOUR EYE CONTACT.** You must also make a conscious effort to look at the audience when you first start. Don't let your nerves make you look at your shoes, the ceiling or the walls. Force yourself to scan the audience and make eye contact with them. Latch onto the ones that look friendly as they will calm your nerves and boost your confidence.

- **DELIVER YOUR FULL PITCH.** Here is your opportunity at last. Now all your careful preparations and many rehearsals, your voice training and control of your body language, are finally going to pay off. You should be able to feel the power that you have as the pitcher and – yes – even enjoy the experience of delivering your presentation and answering questions with confidence.

IMRAN HAKIM OF iTEDDY *set foot in the Den back in Series 4. The pitch may have involved a great big teddy bear with a computer screen in its belly, but the negotiations got serious. Duncan, Deborah and Richard ruled themselves out, leaving just Peter and Theo, who were interested in the content download potential from the iTeddy website. Peter, sensing something exciting in prospect, made an offer for half the money for 22.5%, encouraging Theo to join him in the venture, which Theo agreed to do. The investment was for 45% though, which was three times the amount Imran had offered.*

IMRAN STAYED COOL *as he tried to negotiate down the level of equity Peter and Theo were requesting. With only one deal on the table, Imran had little leverage on the day, but having acknowledged that Peter and Theo would bring a lot to the business, he suggested a figure of 17.5% each. Having suggested this, he then reiterated the figure as the maximum amount of equity he would concede. After some consideration, Peter and Theo relented to come down to 20% each. Judging that he had pushed the negotiations as far as he could, Imran took the deal. Since then, iTeddy has gone on to be one of Dragons' Den's most successful ventures.*

YOUR FINALE

- **HAND OUT THE TAKE-AWAY PACKS.** Only when you've done your presentation and successfully answered all the questions should you bring out the take-away packs. They will probably open their packs and flick through a few pages. They might even study the numbers.

- **ALLOW FOR FINAL QUESTIONS.** Just stand in front of them in the 'relaxed stance' without saying a word. Eventually some of them will look up and you can ask them if they need any more information. Respond to any queries and reiterate any actions that you took to supply more information.

- **CLOSE YOUR PITCH.** At length, take a low deep breath and deliver your closing line looking into their eyes. When you've finished, stand still and let your words just sink in.

ENTERING INTO NEGOTIATIONS

In the Dragons' Den, serious negotiations take place in front of the cameras. In most other settings, though (as mentioned in Commandment 1), it's not that likely you'll get a firm offer of investment on the spot. Usually the investors want time to go through your take-away pack and talk with their experts.

Having said that, someone might bounce a ballpark figure at you to see how you react on the spot. It's at this point that you need to be very determined to hold your ground. In the heat of the moment, you might be tempted to think beyond the minimum amount of money you need and the maximum amount of shares in your business that you had decided you were willing to give away. Don't tell them what your negotiating parameters are, and wait until you have an opening offer on the table before you enter into proper negotiations.

A FINAL THOUGHT

Remember that a pitch is actually a simple process, similar to a job interview. Like a job interview, it may not always have a successful outcome. Indeed, many people say that you won't succeed in business unless you have a few knock-backs and rejections. However, the more you prepare – in the ways described in the Commandments in this book – the more likely you are to deliver a great pitch. Yes, you'll be nervous about the prospect of pitching. Even the most experienced presenters get nerves – but those nerves actually keep you on your toes. Anyone who has made enough preparations and has the right attitude is capable of delivering the perfect pitch.

" THE BEST ADVICE I COULD GIVE TO WOULD-BE ENTREPRENEURS, AND IT IS SOMETHING MY BUSINESS HEROES WOULD AGREE ON, IS THAT ANYONE CAN DO IT "

DUNCAN BANNATYNE, DRAGON

DDN

When Michael Cotton went into the Den in Series 6, he did so representing the four directors of DDN, a company that had designed, patented and produced a device (now known as Fuel Angel) that retrofits onto cars to prevent the driver from putting petrol into a diesel-run car.

MICHAEL DECIDED TO GO IT ALONE IN THE DEN, *rather than take all four directors of DDN. It kept things focused and pegged back the limits of negotiation.*

The fact that Michael was a representative of the four equal directors was a significant factor that came to light during questioning. It was crucial to the deal that was ultimately struck, as the directors had set a tight limit on how much equity they were prepared to give away. Michael's initial offer was for just 20% equity.

Having outlined the need for the product, its benefit to users, the potential market and projected figures for the first year, Michael was aware that there was considerable interest in the Den. He saw that, by declaring that he had only up to 25% of the company to give away, it would allow for only serious offers and speed up the negotiations. The Dragons had to make their offers without the negotiating room they normally enjoy. Having such a small amount of leeway can be a risky strategy – the Dragons might equally have refused to budge from a figure above 25% – but Michael and his fellow directors were sure they had a great product, a wide open market and a good deal for investors.

Peter and Duncan ruled themselves out, but the remaining three all proposed deals. Michael seized the opportunity to have two Dragons on board and accepted a joint offer from Deborah and Theo.

DDN'S FOCUS WAS ON THE RETROFIT MARKET – *selling their product to the owners of diesel vehicles already in use, especially fleet vehicles. However, Michael was receptive to the Dragons' suggestion of looking into licensing the device to car manufacturers as well.*

THE DRAGONS WERE IMPRESSED: *by the product, the market potential and by Michael himself. Michael Cotton's own observations on the negotiations are revealing: "With the other decision makers not available to badger, it brought the negotiating process to a swift conclusion. I believe that the confidence showed in the product, and the research into the marketplace came across, and allowed us to succeed. Pitches that involve two people allow the Dragons to divide and conquer. Picking on the weaker link can expose a product or business weakness, culminating in a lack of self-confidence that can result in you accepting a lesser deal."*

REFERENCE

DOS AND DON'TS

1 **DO PLAN FOR A PASSIONATE, POWERFUL PITCH.** The best form of pitch consists of a presentation, a question and answer session, and all the detail in a take-away pack. This gives you the greatest level of power as the pitcher.

2 **DO RESEARCH YOUR AUDIENCE.** Understand the different motivations of different types of investor, and learn how to appeal to certain types of personalities in your audience.

3 **DON'T RAMBLE WITH YOUR PRESENTATION.** You need to storyboard the content of your presentation and make head-notes about every part of it, so that you won't start rambling and confusing your audience on the day.

4 **DON'T LET YOUR CREDIBILITY CRUMBLE.** The audience will be impressed if you can speak confidently without a script and describe how you'll deliver, but you will lose all credibility if you get your figures wrong. Make sure that your take-away pack has all the necessary facts.

5 **DO BRING IN PRODUCT SAMPLES AND OTHER PROPS.** Tangible objects will be the most memorable part of the pitch for your audience. You can also use visual aids and other forms of prop to liven up your presentation and reinforce the messages you want the audience to absorb.

6 **DO PREPARE FOR QUESTIONING.** Learn how to adopt a neutral expression when you're being asked a question and memorize the answers to questions that are likely to be asked. Also learn how to respond when someone asks about something you haven't memorized.

7 **DON'T UNDERESTIMATE THE POWER OF YOUR VOICE.** With simple breathing and vocal exercises you can train your voice to deliver a truly powerful pitch, full of passion and depth. You will be varying the pace and tone of your speech to hold your audience spellbound.

8 **DO USE POSITIVE BODY LANGUAGE.** You can interpret what your audience is thinking from their body language and you can project a positive image with your own.

9 **DON'T LET NERVES GET THE BETTER OF YOU.** Everyone feels nervous to some degree before a pitch, but with certain mental exercises you can train your mind to overcome these fears.

10 **DO PREPARE FOR THE FULL ORDER OF THE DAY.** The pitch itself may be the main part of your performance, but you must start performing as soon as you enter the premises and to continue performing as you enter into negotiations.

JARGON BUSTER

ANCHOR
The sound or sight of something that you condition in yourself to trigger an emotional state of calm.

ANGEL INVESTOR
Private investor who is interested in getting involved with a business as well as providing capital for it.

AUDITORY PERSON
Someone who finds auditory information easiest to take in.

CHUNKING
Reducing information to soundbites or messages reinforced with props.

CROSS-EYE GAZE
Looking diagonally across someone's eyes rather than staring directly into their eyes.

EQUITY
Percentage of shares in a business.

INVESTMENT BANKER
Banker at a financial institution that deals with raising capital, acquisitions and securities trades.

KINAESTHETIC PERSON
Someone who finds it easiest to understand things they can touch.

POWER STANCE
Upright, open-chested, clench-toed posture that gives an aura of power.

POWER MOVE
Series of yoga movements (shrug, hug, squeeze, stretch) used to release tension before presenting.

POWER OF THREE
The idea that people find a series of three memorable. Can be used to help memorize a speech.

POWERPOINT
Multimedia presentation Software.

PRESENTATION
The giving of information to the audience, usually involving a speech and the use of props. The ideal duration for the presentation in a business pitch is 20 minutes.

PRIVATE EQUITY FIRM
Investment company that pools investor funds to acquire businesses with potential for improved profits and selling on.

RELAXED STANCE
One-legged weighted posture that gives a relaxed, yet alert aura.

Q&A SESSION
Question and answer session between the audience and pitcher.

SOFT-SELL
Selling tactic that draws out the positive emotions rather than logical reactions of an audience.

STORYBOARD
Way of working out the structure of a pitch on paper, by dividing it into boxes or scenes.

TAKE-AWAY PACK
Printed material with all the detailed facts and figures that support your business pitch.

VENTURE CAPITALIST
Professional investor who provides capital in return for equity in companies with high potential growth.

VISUAL PERSON
Someone who finds visual information easiest to understand.

VISUALS
Visual props, usually in the form of boards or projected slides.

CREDITS

Produced by Thameside Media
www.thamesidemedia.com

Creative Director & Photographer:
Michael Ellis
Editorial Director: Rosalyn Ellis
Assistant Photographer:
Sergio Zimerman
Proofreader and Indexer: Zoe Ross

DRAGONS' DEN

Product Director: Lisa O'Connell
Licensing Director: David Christopher

The publishers would like to thank Sam Lewens, Holly Simpson, Helen Bullough and Richard Curwen at the BBC, and the team at 2waytraffic.

Thameside Media would like to thank all the Dragons' Den entrepreneurs who kindly provided their assistance:

Iain McGill and Joe Gill of About Time; Michael Pritchard of Anyway Spray; Ed Wray at BarbeSkew; Richard Enion and Michael Davis of BassToneSlap; Frank Drewett of Bin Lid Lifter; Simeone Salik, Janice Dalton and Dominic Lawrence of Blinds In A Box; Charlotte Evans and Carolyn Jarvis of Buggyboot; Eddie Middleton at Chillchasers; Helen Wooldridge and Polly Marsh of Cuddledry; Julia Charles of D4M; Michael Cotton of DDN; Clive Billing of Diamond Geezer; Josephine Buchan of Dusty; Michael Lea of Earle's Direct; Eglu; Sammy French of Fit Fur Life; Laban Roomes of Goldgenie; Peter Neath and Ian Worton of Grillstream; Eoin O'Mahony at Hamfatter; Alistair Turner at Igloo; Imran Hakim of iTeddy; Joe Reade at Island Bakery Organics; Karen O'Neill and Karen Coombes of KCO Iceblading; Dr Gili Kucci of Kucci Kukui; Geoff and Rob Hill of Ladderbox; Raymond Smith of Magic Pizza; Neil Westwood at Magic Whiteboard; Sharon Wright of Magnamole; David and Patti Bailey of Motormouse; Carol Savage of MyDish; Victoria McGrane of Neurotica; Michael North, The Olive Man; Paul Ward of Paragon PE; Kay Russell of Physicool; Levi Roots of Reggae Reggae Sauce; Paul Tinton of Prowaste; Guy Portelli; Andy Harsley of Rapstrap; Red Button Design; Max McMurdo of Reestore; Samantha Gore of Saboteur; Toby and Oliver Richmond of Servicing Stop; Samantha Fountain of Shewee; Lesley-Ann Simmons of Shoes Galore; Jane Rafter of Slinks; Ronan McCarthy of Spit 'n' Polish Shoeshine; Shaun Pulfrey of Tangle Teezer; Jason Roberts of Tech 21; Rachel Watkyn of Tiny Box Company; Steve Smith of trueCall; Rob Law at Trunki; Sarah Lu of Youdoodoll; Tony Earnshaw of UK Commercial Cleaning; Adejare Doherty of The Wholeleaf Company

Case studies compiled by Thameside Media

For the official Dragons' Den website, see www.bbc.co.uk/dragonsden

PICTURE CREDITS

Jacket photography and chapter opener images of the Dragons' Den by Thameside Media

Images of entrepreneurs' products and premises kindly supplied by the businesses named

Image of Evan Davis, p10, provided by HarperCollins

Additional illustrations pp64, 90, 93, 111, 180 by Thameside Media

FURTHER ADVICE

For the author's website, see www.spalton.co.uk

Business Link provides free business advice and support in the UK
Helpline 0845 600 9006
www.businesslink.gov.uk

ALSO IN THIS SERIES

Dragons' Den: Start Your Own Business (Collins, 2010) ISBN 978-0007364282

Dragons' Den: Grow Your Business (Collins, 2010) ISBN 978-0007364268

FURTHER READING

Dragons' Den: Success, From Pitch To Profit (Collins, 2008) ISBN 978-0007270828

Duncan Bannatyne *Anyone Can Do It: My Story* (Orion, 2007) ISBN 978-0752881898

Duncan Bannatyne *Wake Up and Change Your Life* (Orion, 2009) ISBN 978-0752882871

Duncan Bannatyne *How To Be Smart With Your Money* (Orion, 2009) ISBN 978-1409112860

Duncan Bannatyne *How To Be Smart With Your Time* (Orion, 2010) ISBN 978-1409112884

James Caan *The Real Deal* (Virgin, 2009) ISBN 978-0753515099

Peter Jones *Tycoon* (Hodder, 2008) ISBN 978-0340952351

Deborah Meaden *Common Sense Rules* (Random House, 2010) ISBN 978-1847940278

Theo Paphitis *Enter the Dragon* (Orion, 2009) ISBN 978-0752894225

INDEX